Meatopia

A Meat Odyssey

By

Liane J. Pixley

MEATS

BEEF

Roastbeef

Never wash a raw roast, at least not the parts unprotected by the thin skin. Wipe the skin off with vinegar, dry with a soft cloth, and lay the meat, cut sides at top and bottom, upon the grating of your roaster. Dash a cupful of really boiling water over it. They cicatrice the surface and keep in the juices. Dredge with flour, cover and cook ten minutes to the pound, turning all the heat into the oven for fifteen minutes; then shift into a slower oven, or "dampen" the fire. Baste every ten minutes with the gravy dripping into the pan. Ten minutes before dishing the meat, wash freely with butter and dredge with browned flour, to "glaze" the roast.

Never serve "made gravy" with roast beef. Pour the liquid from the pan into a bowl, and when the fat is solid, remove it and clarify for dripping. The residuum will add richness to your soup-stock, or make a savory base for stew or hash.

Serve horseradish sauce and mustard with your rare roast, and put a little of the ruddy juice which exudes as the meat is carved, upon each slice when served.

RoastbeefwithY orkshirepudding

Fifteen minutes before taking up the roast just described, skim six tablespoonfuls of fat from the gravy, put into a smaller dripping-pan, or pudding-dish, and set in the oven. Have ready this batter:

Sift an even teaspoonful of salt and one of baking-powder twice with a pint of flour. Beat two eggs light, add to them two cupfuls of milk, turn in the sifted flour and mix quickly. Set the reserved fat upon the upper grating of the oven; when it begins to bubble, turn in the batter, and cook quickly to a fine, golden-brown. Cut into squares and garnish the meat with them when you dish it.

This is a better way than cooking the pudding in the roaster under the meat, as used to be the custom with English cooks.

Réchauffé of beef à la jardinière

Lay yesterday's piece of beef in a roasting-pan, sprinkle with salt and pepper, and cover it with thick slices of raw tomatoes. Dash a cupful of boiling water over all, put a close cover on the roaster, and cook in a hot oven for thirty-five minutes. While this is cooking boil tender a pint of green peas, a pint of potatoes—cut into tiny squares—three carrots, also cut small, and ten small onions. Season each vegetable with pepper, salt, and a small bit of butter.

Lay the beef with the tomatoes upon it on a hot platter, pour over it any gravy remaining in the pan, and arrange neatly about it the other vegetables. Be sure that meat and vegetables are very hot when served.

Braised beef

Put a nice round of beef in a broad-bottomed iron pot with a tablespoonful of butter, and sprinkle a chopped onion over it. Cook the beef on one side until brown, then turn and cook on the other side for the same length of time. Now dash a pint of boiling water over the meat, put a close cover on the pot and let the contents cook slowly, allowing at least fifteen minutes to every pound of beef. When the meat is done, remove from the pot to a platter and keep warm while you strain the gravy left in the pot; return to the fire and thicken it with a tablespoonful of browned flour rubbed into the same quantity of butter. Season the gravy with salt, pepper, and a teaspoonful of kitchen bouquet, and pour it over the meat.

Rib-ends of beef

These are usually cut off when the roast is rolled, and can be bought cheap.

Fry in beef fat a sliced onion and a chopped sweet pepper—carefully seeded. Take these up with a skimmer and keep hot. Pepper, salt and flour the rib-ends and fry in the same fat until they begin to brown. Put, now, with the fat into a saucepan, strew the fried onion and pepper on top; pour in a cup of weak stock; fit on a close cover, and cook very slowly until the beef is tender.

Strain and skim the gravy, thicken with browned flour; add a teaspoonful of kitchen bouquet; arrange the beef-bones in a dish; pour the gravy over them and serve.

Pot-roastofcoarsebeef

Cut four pounds of coarse lean beef in one piece. Fry half a pound of fat salt pork in a rather shallow pot. Put in the beef, and cook fast on both sides for five minutes. Cover with a chopped onion and a cupful of canned tomatoes, a sliced carrot and a sliced turnip. Now, pour in enough hot water to come half-way to the top of the meat; cover closely and simmer slowly for two hours, turning at the end of the first hour.

Take out the beef; rub with butter, pepper and salt, and set in the oven while you skim and strain the gravy, rubbing the vegetables with it through a colander. Put this back into the pot, thicken with browned flour, boil up once; pour half over the meat and serve the rest in a gravy-boat.

Rolledboiledbeef

(An English recipe)

Cut an oblong piece of beef from the flank. It should be two inches thick, twelve inches long and six wide. Lay it on a dish and spread upon it this forcemeat:

A cupful of cracker crumbs, two tablespoonfuls of finely-chopped salt pork, half a teaspoonful of salt, one saltspoonful, each, of thyme, marjoram, and sage, half a saltspoonful of pepper, a few drops of onion juice, or one teaspoonful of chopped onion, and one egg. Moisten with a good stock until soft enough to spread over the meat.

Roll as you would a valise pudding, tie about with pack-thread and sew up in mosquito netting or cheese-cloth. Put on in plenty of boiling water and cook slowly for four hours. Let it lie in the water until the latter is a little more than lukewarm, and put under a heavy weight until next day. Remove the cloth, cut the strings and serve cold with horseradish sauce.

Corned beef is very good prepared in this way. Add vinegar to the water in which it is boiled and omit the pork from the stuffing.

Beef à la mode (No. 1)

Cut two pounds of lean beef from the round into strips. Cover the bottom of a pudding-dish with thin strips of bacon, then put in half the meat and strew over this carrots, turnips and onions, sliced very thin. There should be four of these, part of them going over the first layer of beef, the remainder over the second layer of beef. With them go two bay-leaves broken into bits. Cover all with stock, make a paste of flour and water, rolling it out as for pie crust, cover the top of the bake-dish with this, pinching it down about the edges so that no steam may escape. Bake for two hours in a steady oven, remove the paste cover, and send the dish at once to the table.

Beef à la mode (No. 2)

Have a solid piece cut from the round, and tie into shape with stout cords at intervals of an inch apart. Plug the meat perpendicularly with strips of fat salt pork, long enough to project half an inch at top and bottom. Make incisions clear through the beef with a sharp, thin knife, and fill these with forcemeat made of fat pork, minced, onion and bread-crumbs, sharply seasoned. Lay the meat in a braising-pot, cover deep with chopped onion, carrot, turnip, celery, three bay-leaves, a sliced tomato, and sprinkle with mace and paprika. Now pour in a cupful of cold water, cover closely and cook slowly fifteen minutes to the pound.

If you wish to serve hot, clip the threads; rub the gravy through a colander, let it cool a few minutes to throw up the fat; skim and thicken with browned flour, and pour half over the meat, half into a gravy-boat.

It is, however, nicer if left to get cold in the gravy, with a heavy weight on top, until next day. Then remove the cords, and cut in thin, horizontal slices.

An underdone roast can be metamorphosed in this way for a second-day's dinner.

Braised rolled beefsteak

This is a good way of dealing with a hopelessly tough steak. Lay upon a board and pound from end to end with a mallet. Cover with a forcemeat of minced salt pork, onion and seasoned crumbs, wet with a little gravy; roll up upon the stuffing and tie into shape. Lay in your roaster; pour in a little cold water (or, better still, weak stock), cover and cook slowly for two hours, basting often with gravy from the pan. Undo the strings carefully, after pinning the roll together with skewers, and lay upon a hot dish, covered, while you prepare the gravy. Skim, thicken with browned flour, add a good spoonful of kitchen bouquet, boil up and pour into a boat.

Baked beefsteak à la jardinière

Still another way of making a tough steak eatable. Pound it on both sides and lay in lemon juice and salad oil for two hours. Transfer then to your roaster, cover with two sliced tomatoes, a sliced carrot, an onion and a turnip, with minced sweet herbs. Add a cupful of cold water, cover closely and cook slowly twenty minutes to the pound.

Cut one large carrot, two large onions, two turnips and four stalks of celery into neat dice and cook them soft, without break ing, in salted water, each in a pan of its own. In another saucepan cook four large tomatoes, peeled and whole.

When the steak is done, keep hot over boiling water, while you rub the vegetables with which it was cooked through the colander or a vegetable press back into the gravy, thickening this with browned flour. Boil one minute, add the juice of a lemon and a glass of sherry, and keep hot in a closed vessel. Dish the meat, lay the vegetable dice about it in little heaps, each kind by itself, leaving the tomatoes whole; pour the rich gravy over all; cover the dish and leave in the open oven for three minutes to let the gravy soak in.

You have now a "French dish," that will amply repay the additional pains it has cost you.

A family pot-roast of beef

The round will serve for this dish. Fry slices of fat salt pork in an iron pot, and when crisp, remove and throw in a sliced onion. When this is browned, remove and lay the roast in the pot. Cook for ten minutes, turn and cook for five minutes more. Now, add a cupful of water, cover closely and simmer over a slow fire for an hour. Add a sliced carrot, two teaspoonfuls of lemon juice, a bay-leaf and a tablespoonful of Worcestershire sauce to the contents of the pot. Turn the beef over and over in this, and if the meat seem dry add a cupful of water, or, better still, stock. Cook covered, very slowly, for two hours more. Transfer the meat to a hot platter, thicken the gravy left in the pot with a brown roux, salt and pepper to taste, and stir in two tablespoonfuls of vinegar. Pour this sauce over the meat and send to the table.

A New England pot-roast

Lay a round of beef in a broad, deep pot. Pour in a cupful of boiling water, add two slices of onion, cover closely and cook gently ten minutes to the pound. Transfer to a dripping-pan, rub with butter, dredge with flour, and brown in a quick oven. Strain and cool the gravy left in the pot, take off the fat, put the gravy into a saucepan, season with pepper, salt and a little kitchen bouquet, and thicken with a heaping tablespoonful of brown roux. Boil up once and serve in a gravy-boat, or pour around the base of the beef.

Savory ragout of beef

Cut a round beefsteak into inch-squares. Fry minced salt pork in a pan until you have enough fat to fry the meat, then remove the bits of pork and lay in the meat, each piece of which must first be rolled in flour. When the meat is brown at the edges, add to the fat two tablespoonfuls of flour that has been lightly browned, stir in a pint of weak stock, or, if you have not that, of boiling water; stir to a brown sauce, and return the meat to it, throwing in, at the same time, a minced onion. Leave the meat at the side of the range where it will cook very slowly for three-quarters of an hour. Now, season to taste with salt, add a bay leaf and a little kitchen bouquet. A little Worcestershire sauce is thought by some to be an improvement. Cover again and cook, still slowly, for over an hour, or until the meat is very tender. Stir in two tablespoonfuls of vinegar, and turn out upon a heated platter.

Beefhotpot

Two pounds of beef ribs; one tablespoonful of dripping; two chopped onions and six tiny green peppers, four slices of toast, a little black pepper, chives, vinegar, thyme, raisins, olives, tomatoes to taste, all minced.

Heat the dripping in a saucepan, put into it the ingredients (leave the peppers whole, and mince the chives), cover closely and stew until boiled to rags. Thicken with butter rolled in browned flour. Serve on toast.

Boiledbeeftongue(smoked)

Wash the tongue well and soak four hours in tepid water. Put over the fire in plenty of cold water and cook twelve minutes to the pound after the boil begins. Let it get cold in the water; pare and trim neatly, and garnish with small green pickles.

Braisedfr eshbeef 'stongue(No.1)

Wash the tongue and boil for half an hour. Trim away the root and the tough edges.

Fry a sliced onion in three tablespoonfuls of dripping. Strain out the onion and lay the tongue in the frying-pan. Cook ten minutes, turning twice. Remove to your covered roaster; lay upon the grating and dredge with flour. Pour the fat over it; add a large cupful of boiling water and cook, closely covered, for an hour and a half, basting four times.

Take up and keep hot over boiling water while you skim off the fat, and thicken with browned flour. Season with paprika, onion juice, salt and half a cupful of strained tomato sauce.

Dish the tongue and pour the gravy over it. Send around horseradish sauce with it.

Sauce for braised tongue

Cook together in a saucepan a tablespoonful, each, of butter and flour until they bubble. Into a half-pint cup put a couple of teaspoonfuls of vinegar, fill up the cup with boiling water, and turn this on the butter and flour. Stir until thick and smooth. Just before taking from the fire stir in a tablespoonful of grated horseradish. Let it get hot, and serve.

Braised fresh tongue (No. 2)

Clean, and boil for an hour, leaving in the water for fifteen minutes after taking it from the fire. Trim neatly. Skewer the tip and root of the tongue together and lay in your covered roaster upon a layer of sliced onion, carrot, celery, tomatoes, and minced parsley. Cover with the same; add a cupful of the water in which the tongue was boiled, fit on your cover and cook slowly for two hours. Dish the tongue and keep hot. Rub gravy and vegetables through the colander, into a saucepan; thicken with browned flour. Lay the tongue in a bake-pan; pour the gravy over it, and set upon the top grating of an oven to brown. Dish, pour the gravy about the tongue and serve. Eat mushroom sauce with it.

Mushroom sauce for the above

Wash the mushrooms, wipe and peel them, then cut into tiny dice. Stir in a little of the gravy from the tongue; season with salt and paprika; add a lump of butter rolled in browned flour and cook two minutes.

A little lemon juice improves the flavor.

An Italian entrée of beef's tongue

This is a good way to warm up the remains of a boiled or roast fresh tongue. Slice, cover with oil and lemon-juice, and leave in the marinade for one hour. Then add salt, pepper, some sliced onion, a little parsley and a few mushrooms cut into halves. Place in a frying-pan and cook slowly for about fifteen minutes, moistening with a tablespoonful of sherry and a little lemon juice; just before taking from the fire add a little brown stock, and a little tomato sauce, well-seasoned.

Boiledbeef 'stongue

Wash well and cook in salted, boiling water until a steel skewer goes easily into the thickest part. Leave in the water for fifteen minutes, trim, and lay on a hot dish. Pour sauce tartare over it and send more around with it.

Boiledbeef 'sheart

Wash the heart and soak for half an hour in cold, salted water. Wipe and stuff the ventricles with a forcemeat of bread-crumbs and chopped ham or salt pork, minced fine and well seasoned. Sew up in cheese-cloth fitted to the heart, and bring slowly to a boil in salted water, to which a tablespoon of vinegar has been added. Boil gently two hours, turning the heart several times.

Remove the cloth and dish the heart. Pour a piquante sauce over it.

The heart is made more savory if you will boil it in weak stock instead of water.

Roastbeef 'sheart

Prepare as directed in last recipe, but roast instead of boiling, laying the heart upon a bed of minced onion and tomatoes, and pouring in a little hot water to make the gravy. Rub this through a colander, thicken with browned flour, season to taste and pour over the heart.

Howtocornbeef

Mix salt with saltpeter in the proportion of ten parts of the first to one of the second, and with this rub the piece of beef to be corned until the salt lies dry upon the surface. Let it stand in a cold place for twenty-four hours and repeat the process, and the next day put it into pickle. This is made by boiling together for ten minutes a gallon of salt, four ounces of saltpeter, and a pound and a half of brown sugar in five gallons of water. The meat should not be put into the pickle until the latter is perfectly cold. Leave it in the pickle and take it out as needed, looking after it once in a while to see if it is keeping well. If not, take the meat out, rub it well with dry salt, and prepare a fresh and stronger brine.

Howtocornatongue

Put into a saucepan a gallon and a half of water, a half-pound of brown sugar, two and a quarter ounces of salt and a half-ounce of saltpeter. Boil for half an hour, skim and, when cold, pour over the tongue.

It should be ready for use in a week.

Boiledcornedbeef

Soak for an hour in cold water. Put over the fire in plenty of cold water. Put into the pot with it a peeled carrot and a small onion, and for a gallon of water a tablespoonful of vinegar. Cook slowly, allowing twenty-five minutes to the pound if very salt, or if the meat has lain in the brine for some weeks. Let it lie in the liquor for half an hour after it is done. Lift it then, trim away ragged edges, lay on a hot dish and wash all over with butter in which has been beaten the juice of half a lemon.

Strain a cupful of the liquor; stir into it a tablespoonful of butter rolled in one of flour, boil two minutes and add a great spoonful of minced pickles, or of capers. Some like to use pickled onions for this purpose.

Send around horseradish and mustard with it.

When it leaves the table put a plate with a heavy weight upon it, and leave thus all night.

VEAL

Roast leg of veal

Wipe a leg of veal with a damp cloth and place it in a covered roaster. Dash a cupful of boiling water over the meat, cover it closely and cook at the rate of twenty minutes to the pound. Half an hour before the meat is taken from the oven remove the cover from the roaster, baste the meat with the gravy in the pan, and brown.

Shoulder of veal

This may be roasted, like the leg, but is better for having the bone removed, and the cavity thus left filled with a forcemeat made of bread-crumbs and chopped ham, seasoned to taste.

Veal cutlets

Wipe the cutlets with a damp cloth, dip them, first, in beaten egg, then in cracker dust, and set in a cold place for an hour. Fry in dripping to a rich brown. Cook slowly that they may be thoroughly done. Lay for a moment on brown paper to drain free of grease, and put on a hot platter. Serve with tomato sauce.

Veal steaks with mushroom sauce

Broil the steaks slowly over a clear fire, turning often that they may not scorch. When done, keep the meat hot on a platter in the oven while you make the following sauce:

Drain the liquor from a can of mushrooms and cut the mushrooms in halves. Cook together a tablespoonful of butter and one of browned flour until they are dark brown in color. Pour upon them the mushroom liquor and a cupful of beef stock. Stir to a smooth sauce, season with a dash of Worcestershire sauce, salt and pepper, and add the halved mushrooms. Cook for two minutes, stirring constantly, then pour over and around the veal steaks.

Breast of veal á la jardiniére

Lard with strips of fat salt pork, and sprinkle with paprika. Dredge with flour and lay upon the grating of your covered roaster, add enough boiling water to cover it barely, and roast for an hour, basting with the gravy every ten or fifteen minutes. Then turn on the other side and spread over the roast a pint of tomatoes peeled and sliced, two onions, chopped fine, two sprigs of parsley, chopped fine, and two chopped peppers. Baste for another hour every ten minutes. When the meat is removed keep hot while you take up the vegetables with a split spoon, and keep them hot also. Strain the gravy, thicken with browned flour, and put into a boat. Lay the vegetables about the meat upon a metal or fire-proof dish, dredge this last with browned crumbs, and dot with softened butter. Set upon the top grating of the oven for five minutes to brown and send to table in the dish.

Stuffed roast fillet of veal

Take out the central bone and skewer the fillet into a neat round. Make a forcemeat of crumbs, minced pork, onion juice, parsley and half a can of mushrooms, minced. Wet with a few spoonfuls of stock or gravy; fill the bone-hole and ram the stuffing into the folds of the meat from both sides. Lay on your covered roaster, cover with very thin slices of fat salt pork, and dash a cupful of boiling water over top and sides. Roast, covered, twelve minutes to the pound. Fifteen minutes before you draw it from the oven remove the pork, wash with butter and dredge with browned flour. Then brown, uncovered.

The fillet should be basted four times while roasting. After the fourth basting draw off a cupful of gravy from the dripping-pan, set on ice, or in cold water until the fat rises, skim, add four tablespoonfuls of strained tomato juice, thicken with browned flour, and cook three minutes before pouring into a gravy-boat.

Roast breast of veal

Cook as you would the fillet, running a sharp knife between ribs and meat to make space for the stuffing.

Serve spinach with it.

Breaded veal cutlets

Roll the cutlets in fine crumbs, salted and peppered; dip into beaten egg, then again in crumbs. Set on ice for an hour to get firm, and fry in deep fat, turning three times, carefully. Cook slowly after the first five minutes. Underdone veal is unwholesome and unpalatable.

Drain off the fat, and serve in a heated dish. Send around horseradish or tomato sauce with them, and accompany with spinach.

Mock squabs

Have six or eight slices cut from a loin of veal, half an inch thick, about seven inches long and four wide. Make a forcemeat of crumbs, fat pork, and minced mushrooms seasoned with paprika, onion juice and a little lemon juice with a suspicion of grated lemon-peel. Moisten with a beaten egg and cover with this each slice of meat nearly to the edge, roll up tightly and tie with twine, or fasten with wooden skewers. Dredge with salt, pepper and flour, roast them as previously directed, golden-brown. Be very careful that they do not brown or become too highly colored. When nearly done add cream to almost cover and let them simmer about fifteen minutes or until quite tender. Remove the strings, arrange the "squabs" on toast, garnish with water-cress, and pour a little of the strained cream over each. Serve with asparagus or spinach.

Larded veal

Have a solid piece cut from the thickest part of the shoulder. Lard at short intervals with strips of fat salt pork and put into your covered roaster with sliced carrot, onion, bits of celery and a few sprigs of parsley; over all pour a large cupful of good stock, cover and cook slowly for about three hours. You should baste frequently while cooking, and a short time before it is done remove the cover, to cook the larding thoroughly and give a good color to the veal.

Just before taking up pour out a cupful of gravy, skim off the fat and thicken with browned flour, add a great spoonful of tomato catsup, and simmer until you are ready to dish the meat. Pour then into a boat.

Roastcalves'hearts

You will need two hearts for a dish of moderate size. Wash them thoroughly, leaving in salt and water for an hour, to draw out the blood. Run a slender, keen knife from the large end of each heart straight to the center, turning it around several times to make a central hole for the forcemeat stuffing. Make this of cracker crumbs highly seasoned with onion juice, salt and pepper, thyme or marjoram. Moisten with melted butter, or use hot water and a little fat pork or bacon finely chopped. Sew the opening together, and thrust in several lardoons of salt pork. Dredge with salt, pepper and flour. Fry one sliced onion in dripping in a frying-pan. Put in the heart and brown it lightly all over. Pour in stock to cover it—barely—add a bay leaf, two slices of carrot and one teaspoonful of salt. Cover the pan and cook in a moderate oven about two hours, or until very tender.

VEAL AND BEEF
ROAST BEEF
VEAL CHOPS AND SPINACH
MOCK PIGEONS
BOILED CALF'S HEAD

When done remove the strings, put the hearts upon a hot dish, and thicken the gravy with browned flour. Add lemon juice and other seasoning if needed. Strain over the hearts. Garnish with Parisian potatoes alternately with small tomatoes, pared and baked. Pour melted butter and minced parsley over potatoes and tomatoes.

Larded liver

Wash a calf's or lamb's liver, lard it with narrow strips of salt pork, and put it into a covered roaster. Pour over the liver a pint of cold beef stock and cover the pan closely. Set in a moderate oven and cook an hour and a half. Transfer the liver to a deep dish and put the pan containing the gravy on the top of the range. Thicken the gravy with a heaping tablespoonful of browned flour and add to it a cupful of strained tomato liquor, a teaspoonful of onion juice, salt and pepper to taste. Boil up once and pour over the liver.

Salmi of liver

Boil a calf's liver for one hour in slightly salted water, and let it get cold. Cut into dice of uniform size, and for each cupful allow one tablespoonful of butter, one cupful of stock, one teaspoonful of tomato sauce, and two tablespoonfuls of chopped olives. Brown the butter, add one tablespoonful of flour and brown again; add gradually the stock, and stir until smooth and thick. Put in the catsup, olives and liver dice, season to taste, and simmer for fifteen minutes. Serve hot.

A delightful and not inelegant *entrée*.

Roast sweetbreads

Parboil two pairs of sweetbreads and blanch by throwing them into cold water. Drain, pierce three or four holes in each and press into these holes narrow strips of fat salt pork, allowing the strips to project a half-inch on each side. Lay the sweetbreads in a roasting-pan, pour a cupful of weak veal stock over them and rub them with melted butter. Cover and bake for twenty-five minutes; remove from the pan, sprinkle with salt and pepper, put a spoonful of the thickened and seasoned gravy upon each, and send to the table.

Bakedcalf 'shead

The head should be cleaned with the skin left on, also the ears, and split down the under side, leaving the top unbroken. Remove the tongue and brains, parboil and set them on ice. Put the head on in plenty of cold water, boil quickly and for one minute after the boiling point is reached. Take the head off and lay in ice-cold water. Change this for colder in ten minutes, and leave in this for several hours.

Then put over the fire in boiling water, to which a tablespoonful of vinegar has been added, and a tablespoonful of salt. Cook gently until you can slip out the bones easily.

Do this, drawing the teeth, cheek-bones and skull, taking care not to break the upper skin. Put into a bake-dish, restoring the shape as well as you can. Cut the tongue into slices and lay close against the cheeks; wash plentifully with butter rubbed to a cream with lemon juice, sift dry crumbs all over it and bake, covered, half an hour. Then brown.

To make the gravy, rub the brains to a soft paste; pepper and salt, season with tomato catsup and onion juice, add enough of the liquor in which the head was boiled to make a boatful of gravy, thicken with butter rolled in flour, simmer five minutes and serve.

There is no more savory preparation of calf's head than this. It goes to table in the bake-dish. The liquor from the pot in which it had the second boiling makes excellent soup stock.

Boiled calf's head

Boil as directed in last recipe, but do not blanch or bone. When it has been cooked tender, dish, with the tongue (which should have been boiled with it), sliced and laid against the cheeks, and pour over it a brain gravy, made as for the baked head, with the addition of a great spoonful of minced olives.

Mockturtle

Boil and blanch a calf's head, take out the bones and let the meat and tongue get cold in the liquor. Do not let it remain long enough to jelly. As soon as the meat is firm take it from the stock, wipe dry, and cut with the tongue into neat dice an inch long, and half as wide. Make a gravy of a large cupful of the pot liquor, thickened with butter rolled in browned flour and seasoned with lemon and onion juice, a teaspoonful of kitchen bouquet, a little salt and paprika. Put in the meat, and simmer fifteen minutes.

Have ready a sauce made by heating a cupful of cream (adding a pinch of soda) and pour it, stirring all the time, upon the beaten yolks of three eggs. Stir and beat for one minute, and add to the meat and gravy. Now add a glass of sherry and pour all into a deep dish, in which you have laid a pile of turtle eggs made by rubbing together the yolks of three hard-boiled eggs and the boiled brains of the calf, binding them with a raw egg and a little browned flour. They should be made into little marbles with floured hands and cooked in boiling butter for two minutes, then fished out and drained in a colander.

A delicious *entrée*!

Calf's liver á la jardiniére

Lard a large liver with strips of fat salt pork. Cover the bottom of a large saucepan with a carrot and a young turnip (all cut into dice), six very small onions, a handful of green peas and the same of string beans cut into short lengths. Lay the liver upon these, pepper it and pour in a cupful of stock, or a cupful of hot water in which a tablespoonful of butter has been melted. Cover closely and cook an hour and a half without opening. In a bake-pan cook four peeled tomatoes of medium size. Take up the liver and the vegetables, the latter with a split spoon. Lay the liver upon a hot dish, group the vegetables (the tomatoes included), each of a kind together, about it; keep hot in the oven while you strain the gravy into a saucepan, add a great spoonful of catsup and a tablespoonful of browned flour wet with cold water, and cook for one minute. Pour a few spoonfuls over liver and vegetables, the rest into a boat.

Casserole of calf 's liver

Wash and wipe a calf's liver perfectly dry. Fry a few slices of fat bacon in a pan until the fat is all fried out. Strain and return the fat to the pan, lay in the liver and fry two minutes on each side, and then put into the casserole; add one pint of rich brown sauce, a cupful of button onions that have been browned in butter and three tablespoonfuls of lemon juice. Fasten on the cover with a flour and water paste, put in a moderate, steady oven, and cook for two hours. Then remove the paste from the cover, put in potato balls that have been fried in hot fat, and send to the table in the casserole.

Fried brains for garnishing

Soak the brains in cold water for an hour, cover with fresh, cold water and bring to a boil. Cook for three minutes; drain, and set in a cold place for an hour. Cut in thick slices, sprinkle with salt and white pepper; dip in beaten egg, roll in cracker dust and set in a cold place long enough for the coating to stiffen. Fry in deep cottolene or other fat.

Scallop of calf 's brain

Soak brains in cold water for an hour, then boil for ten minutes. Drop into iced water, and when very cold cut into tiny dice. Butter a pudding dish, put in a layer of the brains, sprinkle with pepper, bits of butter and a few drops of onion juice; then put in a thin layer of minced ham. Add more brains, and proceed in this way until the dish is full. Sprinkle the top with buttered crumbs, pour a cupful of veal stock over all, and bake for twenty minutes.

Brain croquettes for garnishing

Prepare the brains as in the preceding recipe, chop and add to them butter, salt and pepper to taste. Into each cupful of the mixture stir a tablespoonful of crumbs and moisten all with cream. Heat in a double boiler, and when the boiling point is reached whip in slowly a beaten egg, and remove the mixture from the fire. Turn upon a dish to cool and stiffen before forming into small croquettes. Crumb these and set on the ice for two hours. Fry in deep, boiling cottolene or other fat.

Any dish of liver or calf's head—in fact of veal in any form—is made elegant by a garnish of brains, fried as croquettes, or in slices.

MUTTON

Roast leg of mutton with sorrel sauce

Wipe a leg of young mutton with a damp cloth, then with a dry. Put into a covered roaster, dash a cupful of boiling water over it and roast at the rate of twelve minutes to each pound of the meat. Fifteen minutes before serving remove the cover and brown. If you do not use a covered roaster baste the meat every fifteen minutes, while cooking, with the gravy in the pan.

Do not send made mutton gravy to the table with it. Pass currant jelly with it and such a sauce as this:

Mince a cupful of field sorrel—young and tender—and stir two tablespoonfuls of butter rubbed into one of browned flour into a cupful of boiling water. Add the sorrel, a dash of paprika and salt. Cook for one minute, take from the fire and beat into it, a very little at a time, the well-whipped yolk of an egg. Set in boiling water until the mutton is served. It must not cook.

Boiled leg of mutton

Carefully trim the meat, cutting off all loose or gristly portions, and wipe with a damp cloth. Have a kettle of boiling water and put in the meat, boiling fast for about ten minutes, when it may simmer until done. Do not put in salt or pepper until nearly cooked. Eat with caper sauce.

The water in which the mutton is boiled makes excellent Scotch broth, or plain mutton soup.

Roast shoulder of mutton

Carefully remove the bone, or shoulder blade, and fill the place with this forcemeat: One cupful of fine bread-crumbs, one tablespoonful of chopped parsley, one teaspoonful of chopped onion, salt and pepper to taste, a half-dozen chopped mushrooms—canned or fresh—and melted butter to moisten the mixture. Sew up the slit left by the bone, and place in the covered roaster with a cupful of water or weak stock. Cook quickly at first, basting often, and allowing for cooking about fifteen minutes to the pound. Serve with sorrel or other meat sauce, never with made gravy.

Pass string-beans, tomatoes, green peas or young turnips with it.

Stuffed shoulder of lamb

Have the bone extracted neatly, and fill the cavity left with a stuffing of a cupful of bread-crumbs, a dozen raw oysters, chopped fine, two tablespoonfuls of butter, melted, one tablespoonful of chopped parsley, one teaspoonful of onion juice, one-half teaspoonful of paprika. Roast in a quick oven. Into two tablespoonfuls of softened butter mix one tablespoonful, each, of chopped parsley, onion and lemon juice, and kitchen bouquet. Draw the meat, when done, from the oven, spread it with this prepared sauce, and return to the oven for four minutes. Garnish with small, round, fried potatoes.

Send around green peas with it.

Hotch-potch

Cut two pounds of *lean* mutton into neat pieces an inch square. Peel and slice six medium-sized potatoes, cut into dice, and parboil for five minutes. Parboil also a dozen small, young onions, no larger than the end of your thumb. Have a couple of kidneys—calf's or lamb's—cut into dice, and drain the liquor from fifteen small oysters. Put a layer of meat dice in the dish, then a layer of onions, kidneys and potatoes. Season each layer of vegetables with pepper and salt. Then another layer of meat, onions and kidneys, and the remaining potatoes. Pour on a cupful of hot water, cover the pan closely and bake it in a moderate oven for three hours. Look at it occasionally and add more water if it seems dry.

When nearly ready to serve take up the mixture with a skimmer, arrange it in a deep hot dish. Add the oysters to the gravy left in the pan, cook till they ruffle, add more seasoning if needed, and pour it over the whole.

Familystewoflambandpeas

Cut two pounds of coarse *lean* lamb into dice. There must be neither fat nor bone in it. Fry a sliced onion brown in two tablespoonfuls of dripping or butter. Strain the fat back into the pan, dredge the meat with flour and fry for three minutes in it, turning to sear both sides. Turn meat and fat into a saucepan, add a cupful of stock or of butter and water, cover closely and stew for an hour, or until the lamb is tender. Put in then a cupful of green peas with three leaves of green mint. Cover again and cook until the peas are tender, but not until they break. Have ready a broad dish lined with slices of toast soaked in tomato sauce. Take up meat and peas in a perforated skimmer and lay upon the toast. Keep hot, while you thicken the gravy left in the pot with a tablespoonful of butter rolled in one of browned flour; season, boil up and pour over the stew. Let it stand one minute and serve.

Casseroleoflambchops

Trim two pounds of lean chops and proceed as with the meat in last recipe until they have been browned in the fat.

Now turn meat and fat into your casserole, in the bottom of which is a layer of pared and sliced tomatoes. Have ready half a cupful of potato balls cut with a "gouge" and parboiled for five minutes, a dozen button onions, also parboiled, and half a can of champignons (mushrooms). Sprinkle these over and between the chops. Pour in a cupful of good stock, or gravy, well seasoned; lastly, another layer of sliced tomatoes, salted, peppered, sprinkled with sugar and dotted with butter. Cover the casserole and set in a moderate oven for two hours.

Drain off all the gravy without disturbing the rest of the contents of the casserole. Skim, thicken with browned flour, add the juice of half a lemon, boil up, pour in a glass of sherry, pour gently back into the casserole, cover, set in the oven for three minutes and send to table, covered.

If you once try this recipe you will not be satisfied until the dish it represents becomes a frequent visitor to your table.

MEATANDPOUL TRYPIES

Chickenpie

Cut at every joint a pair of *young* chickens. Lay on ice while you make a gravy of the pinions, necks and feet—scalding and skinning the feet before putting with the rest over the fire, covering deep with cold water and bringing slowly to the boil. Cook until the flesh is in rags, and the liquor reduced by one-half. Strain, season highly with onion juice, salt and paprika, thicken with browned flour and let the gravy get cold.

Meanwhile, arrange your chicken in a bake-dish; lay among the pieces either well-seasoned forcemeat balls no larger than marbles, made of bread-crumbs and hard-boiled yolks, bound with a raw egg, or canned mushrooms. Of course, fresh mushrooms are better if you can afford them. Put in a cupful of cold water, cover with a good crust, half an inch thick, and bake for an hour and a half. Lay a piece of stout paper over the pie to keep it from browning too fast. When you remove this at the end of an hour draw the pie to the door of the oven, fit a funnel into a slit left in the center of the crust and pour in all the gravy it will hold. Do this very quickly, shut up the oven and leave the pie in until done. Remove the paper ten minutes before the time is up and brown lightly.

GAME PIE IN NAPKINED DISH
SMALL CHICKEN PIE
CHICKEN PIE IN SILVER STAND

Cold chicken pie

Make precisely as in last recipe, but add to the gravy while hot a tablespoonful of gelatine soaked for two hours in cold water enough to cover it. Pour into the pie as already directed. Let the pie get cold before eating it. The gravy will be jellied.

This is a nice dish for Sunday dinners in hot weather.

Fowl pie

Cut an old fowl into joints, splitting the back and dividing the breast into quarters. Put over the fire in plenty of cold water, season with onion juice and the juice of half a lemon. No salt and no pepper. Cover closely and simmer very gently for several hours until you find it tender. Strain off the gravy and season with onion juice, celery salt, a bay-leaf, minced parsley, paprika and salt. Return the gravy to the fire, stir in a lump of butter rolled in browned flour and cook one minute. Arrange the chicken in a deep bake-dish, pour in the gravy, lay over the top two hard-boiled eggs cut into thin slices, cover with a good crust, and bake.

Chicken pot pies

For these have several stoneware or other fire-proof deep dishes, about the size of a bird bath. Cut up a young fowl into joints, cover with cold water and cook tender, but not until the meat leaves the bones. Lay a piece of dark meat and one of light in each dish; sprinkle with minced salt pork, and drop in each dish potato marbles which have been parboiled for ten minutes. Add small cubes of pastry, three to each dish, and two small young onions, no bigger than the end of your thumb. Unless they are mere infants, parboil them five minutes before they go in. Have ready two cupfuls of the liquor in which the chicken was cooked. Thicken with a lump of butter rolled in browned flour; season with paprika and minced parsley. The pork should salt it sufficiently. Fill the dishes, cover each with a good crust, make a slit in the middle and bake, covered with paper, half an hour. Then brown.

You may, if you like, make one dish of this, but many prefer the individual "portions."

Chicken and ham pie

Cut up and stew the chickens, as in last recipe. Have ready four good-sized slices of corned ham (not smoked), boiled and cold, and cut into strips. Put a layer of ham in the bottom of a buttered bake-dish, season with chopped mushrooms and parsley, salt and pepper, and add a layer of white sauce, the base of which is the liquor in which the chickens were cooked. Next, place in the dish the pieces of chicken in regular order, and upon these the yolks of hard-boiled eggs. Repeat the seasoning and the sauce, lay a few strips of ham over the top, cover with a good paste, wash the pie with beaten egg, and bake for an hour and a half. If you have no mushrooms you may substitute a little mushroom catsup.

Veal pie (No. 1)

Cut three pounds of lean veal into inch-square cubes; put into a saucepan with a cupful of cold water, and heat slowly. Remove the scum as it begins to boil; add two small onions, sliced, two tablespoonfuls of carrot cubes, and one teaspoonful of salt. Let it simmer until very tender. Put the meat then into a deep baking-dish.

Let the liquor boil down to one cupful and a half, strain it and remove most of the fat. Add one-half cupful of cream or of rich milk, and pepper to taste. Thicken it with a tablespoonful of flour rubbed in one of butter; cook it five minutes, and strain it over the meat. If you have any cold boiled ham you may add a little of it to the veal, cutting it into tiny pieces.

Cover with a rich biscuit dough, half an inch thick, and bake one hour, covered with thick paper. Uncover and brown.

Veal pie (No. 2)

Cut two pounds of coarse lean veal into cubes and cook tender in enough cold water to cover it. Have ready half a pound of finely-minced pork, an onion, chopped fine, two tablespoonfuls of finely-minced olives, a stalk of celery cut fine, and a tablespoonful of chopped parsley. Put a stratum of veal in the bottom of a buttered bake-dish; cover with this mixture and sprinkle with paprika and with butter. When all the materials are used up in this order fill the dish with gravy made by thickening the liquor in which the veal was stewed with browned flour, adding a tablespoonful of tomato catsup, and boiling one minute. Cover with a good crust; make a slit in the top and bake, covered, one hour; then brown.

Beef and tomato pie

Cut a pint of cold roast beef into small dice of uniform size, and mix with it two or three slices of bacon, also cut small. Line a deep dish with good puff paste, put a layer of the beef and bacon in the bottom of the dish, season with pepper and salt, cover with a layer of peeled and sliced tomatoes. Sprinkle with salt and pepper and dots of butter rolled in flour; add more meat and more tomatoes, until the dish is full. Cover the top layer with bits of butter, then with a crust of puff paste, making holes in this for the escape of steam. Bake until brown.

Beef and potato pie

Moisten three cupfuls of minced roast beef with a little stock, season to taste, and put it into a greased pudding-dish. Into a large cupful of mashed potatoes beat a little milk and a tablespoonful of melted butter. Season this potato and spread it over the top of the minced beef. Set it in the oven and bake, covered, for twenty minutes; uncover, wash over with beaten white of eggs and cook for fifteen minutes longer, or until it is lightly browned.

Beefsteak pie

Cut two pounds of round steak into small squares. Cover (barely) with cold water and cook tender, very slowly. Cut two veal kidneys into cubes and (if you can get it) a sweetbread, blanched by throwing it into cold water, after parboiling it. Drain the liquor from the beef, and let both get almost cold. Make a good gravy by thickening this liquor with a tablespoonful of butter rolled in browned flour, seasoning well with kitchen bouquet, onion juice, salt and pepper. Let it simmer two minutes. Arrange the beef, kidneys and sweetbread in neat layers in the dish, interspersing these with a dozen small oysters. Pour in the gravy, cover with a good crust, half an inch thick, and cook, covered, one hour; then brown.

Kidney pie

Cut four kidneys into neat squares and stew gently in weak stock for half an hour. Cook a quarter-pound of macaroni till tender, and cut it into inch lengths. Butter a baking-dish and put in a layer of macaroni; over that spread a layer of sliced kidneys, seasoned with pepper, salt and made mustard. Sprinkle over a little flour, and add a layer of tomatoes. Repeat these layers and cover with fine bread-crumbs when the dish is filled. Pour in a rich gravy made from the stock in which the kidneys were stewed; put small bits of butter over the crumbs on top, and bake steadily for one hour.

Sweetbread pie

Blanch two sweetbreads by parboiling for ten minutes, then leaving in ice-cold water for the same length of time. When firm cut into half-inch squares. Make a white roux by cooking in a saucepan two tablespoonfuls of flour in two of butter, add gradually a cupful of cream heated with a pinch of soda, season with half a teaspoonful of salt and half a saltspoonful of white pepper, a few grains of cayenne, and two tablespoonfuls of stewed and strained tomato. Put the sweetbreads and sauce into a deep dish, cover with a rich crust, make a slit in the center; bake, covered, half an hour, then brown. Beat one egg, add half a cupful of hot cream, and pour into the opening in the crust just before serving.

Mutton chop pie

Trim two pounds of tender chops by cutting away skin, fat, and two inches of the rib bone. With the refuse trimmings make a gravy by cooking slowly three hours in just enough water to cover them. Let it cool, skim off all the fat, season highly, thicken well with browned flour, boil up once and again let it cool.

Arrange the chops on the inside of a bake-dish, overlapping one another; fill the central space with chopped mushrooms, a chopped tomato, six small button onions and a pint of green peas. Pour in the gravy; cover with a good crust, make a slit in the middle and bake, covered, half an hour; then brown.

Veal chop pie

May be made as above, substituting chopped tomatoes for the green peas. In this case have the gravy very thick, as the tomato juice will thin it.

Small pork pies

(A Devonshire recipe.)

Chop fine a quarter of a pound of beef kidney suet and mix with it an equal quantity of butter. Rub both into a pound of flour and set all over the fire in a saucepan until the butter and suet are melted and the flour very hot. Knead together then into a stiff paste, cover with the cloth and put it near the fire while you make ready the meat. There should be about two pounds of the neck of pork, and this should be cut into very small pieces, seasoned liberally with salt, pepper and a teaspoonful of powdered sage, and cooked gently for twenty-five minutes before it goes into the pie. The paste must then be divided into as many pieces as you wish to have pies, and these must be made into round shapes—"built up" into the shape of round pies. The way to do this must be studied carefully, for it is a knack in itself. The fist is put into the middle of the piece of dough from which the pie is to be raised, and by working it in a circular fashion the hollow is formed which is to receive the meat. The process should really be seen to be adequately understood. When the pie is "raised" the meat is put into it, a round of paste laid on the top and its edge pinched to that of the lower crust. It is then baked in a steady, rather slow, oven.

An English pork pie

Cook two pounds of lean pork for half an hour in enough weak stock to cover it. Let it get cold in the liquor (which reserve for the gravy). Take out the cold meat and cut into neat dice. Butter a deep dish and lay in some of the meat. Cover with a layer of hard-boiled eggs, chopped coarsely; season with onion juice, pepper, salt and a pinch of nutmeg. Stick bits of butter here and there. Dust with browned flour.

Strain and reheat the liquor in which the meat was cooked; stir in a lump of butter rolled in browned flour, cook one minute, add a teaspoonful of Worcestershire sauce; pour into the pie, and let it cool before covering with a good paste. Cut a slit in the middle of the crust; bake, covered, three-quarters of an hour. Uncover, wash with white of egg and brown.

Send around apple sauce with it.

A New England pork pie

Boil half a pound of "streaked" salt pork with a sliced onion and four parsnips of moderate size. Put them on in enough cold water to cover them, and boil until the parsnips are tender, the onion cooked to rags. Have ready three fair-sized potatoes, sliced and parboiled. Slice the parsnips. Cut the pork into very small, thin slices, and line a deep dish with it. Put in a layer of sliced potatoes, sprinkle with flour, salt and pepper, a layer of sliced parsnips, then another layer of each. Add enough of the water in which the pork and parsnips were boiled to fill the dish. Cover with a good crust, and bake in a good oven one hour.

It is said by those who like parsnips to be very good—considering!

Pigeon pie

Dress, draw and singe carefully four young pigeons; stuff them with the chopped livers, hearts and gizzards and fine crumbs, mixed with chopped parsley, a good lump of butter, pepper and salt. Run a small wooden skewer through the body of each, fastening the wings to the sides. Cover the bottom of your bake-dish with thin strips of corned ham; season with chopped parsley, mushrooms, pepper and salt; over these lay the pigeons; between every two birds put the yolk of an egg boiled hard, and two or three in the center also. Add to the dish sufficient thick brown gravy to cover the pigeons, cover the pie with puff-paste, and bake for an hour and a half.

PORK

Roast pig

Lay the pig, which has been prepared by the butcher, in cold water for fifteen minutes, then wipe dry, inside and out. Make a stuffing as for a turkey, and work into it two beaten eggs. Stuff the pig to his original size and shape. Sew him up, bend his fore legs backward, and his back legs forward under him, and skewer him thus. Dredge him with flour and put it, with a little salted water, into a covered roaster. Roast for an hour and a half; remove the cover, rub the pig well with butter and return the cover, leaving the slide open. At the end of twenty minutes remove the cover again, rub the pig once more with butter, and brown him for ten minutes. Serve very hot with apple sauce.

A pig for roasting should not weigh over six or seven pounds after it is cleaned. If larger, it is gross food. The meat should be as delicate as chicken.

Roast pork

Score the skin until the knife touches the meat under it. Rub into these lines or squares a mixture of fine crumbs seasoned with onion juice, a little grated lemon-peel and the juice of half a lemon, with pepper and salt to taste. Work in well until the stuffing stands out of the cracks. Put into your roaster, with a cupful of hot water under it, and after covering bring quickly to the point at which the water begins to steam. Slacken the heat then, and cook twenty-five minutes to the pound, basting often with its own gravy.

Pour off this gravy twenty minutes before taking the meat up, and set in a bowl of ice to send all the fat to the top. Greasy pork gravy is an offense to the educated palate. Thicken with browned flour.

A better plan is not to attempt to make gravy, but to send around apple sauce alone with the roast.

Chine of pork braised with apples

Instruct your butcher to cut the chine with plenty of meat on both sides of the bone. Sprinkle it well with pepper and salt, and lightly with sage and sweet marjoram. Pare, core and cut into thick slices three large, tart apples. Cover the grating of your roaster with them, strew with sugar and lay the chine upon them. Dot the meat with butter; cover and roast twenty-five minutes to the pound. At the end of that time transfer the meat to a dripping-pan, turning it over that the side which has lain upon the apples may be uppermost. Wash with butter, cover thick with salted and peppered crumbs, and brown upon the upper grating of a hot oven while you make the gravy.

To do this rub the cooked apple and the liquor with them through a colander into a saucepan, add a little hot water, a lump of butter rolled in flour, and, if very tart, a little sugar; pepper and salt to taste, boil up and turn into a boat.

Serve peas, pudding or beans in some shape with the chine.

Pork tenderloins

Broil over a clear, steady fire, turning as often as they begin to drip. Allow twenty minutes, if small; more when large. Lay upon a heated dish, cover with a mixture of butter, lemon juice, onion juice, pepper, salt and a dash of powdered sage. Turn over and over in this as it melts; cover closely and leave over hot water several minutes to let the seasoning sink into the meat.

Serve browned whole potatoes and apple sauce with them.

Boiled ham

Soak eight hours, and scrub it hard with a stiff brush or whisk to get out salt and dirt. Cover with an abundance of cold water, and put into it two tablespoonfuls of vinegar. Heat very gradually. At the end of the first hour it should not have reached the boiling point. Simmer gently four or five hours. Allow twenty minutes to every pound for a corned ham; twenty-five for a smoked. Let it get almost cold in the liquor—entirely cold before you skin it.

Barbecued fresh ham

Score the rind with a sharp knife. Mix one tablespoonful of mustard seed, half a teaspoonful, each, of celery seed and pepper corns with one cupful of sugar, one cupful of vinegar and two cupfuls of water. Let these stand ten minutes, then pour it over the ham. Turn it in this pickle several times during the day. Next morning put the ham into your covered roaster in a slow oven, fat side down, for the first hour. Strain the pickle and keep it hot on the back of the stove. Baste the ham frequently with it and bake four hours, or until tender.

All of the pickle should have been used in basting. Lay the ham upon a heated dish and keep hot over boiling water while you make the gravy. Strain the liquor, thicken with browned flour, add salt to taste, simmer for five minutes and pour part over the meat, the rest into a boat.

Those who are fond of hot fresh pork can not do better than to try this. It is also delicious cold.

Breaded ham

Boil as directed in recipe for boiled ham. When cold, skin and rub all over with flour. Next, brush with beaten egg, sift fine crumbs thickly ever the egg, then more egg and another coat of crumbs. Dust with pepper and brown gradually.

Eat cold, garnished with parsley.

Baked ham

Is seldom really "baked." Boil a ham eighteen minutes to the pound; leave it one hour in the liquor in which it was cooked; take it out and let it get really cold and firm before stripping off the skin. Rub the upper side with white of egg and sift over it bread dust a quarter of an inch thick. Pepper lightly, and set in the oven for half an hour, or until the coating is well shortened by the oozing fat, and of a nice brown. Let it get cold to the very bone before serving it. If you like a suspicion of onion flavoring, wash the surface to be breaded with onion juice before going over it with the white of an egg.

Baked corned ham

Soak over night. In the morning scrub hard and pare away the underside until the meat and fat show red and white. Wash well with vinegar and do not wipe. Lay, skin downward, in your roaster, covering the side you have pared with a thick paste of flour and water. Have ready a mixture of one cupful of cold water and half as much vinegar, a tablespoonful of molasses and one of onion juice. Pour around the ham; cover closely and bake half an hour to the pound, after the water is hot. Baste six times with the liquor in the pan.

Take up, scrape off the paste, remove the skin, dusting instantly and thickly with fine cracker-crumbs to stop the escape of the juices. There should be a cracker crust a quarter-inch thick. Set upon the upper grating to brown.

Stuffed ham

Wash a ham and soak over night; then, with a narrow, sharp blade, remove the bone. Fill the cavity thus left with a forcemeat of bread-crumbs, seasoned with pepper and moistened with a little water in which a spoonful of butter has been melted. Sew the ham up closely in a piece of cheese-cloth and boil until done, allowing twenty minutes to the pound. Leave it in the water until cold, transfer to a platter and put under a heavy weight for twelve hours. Now remove the cloth and the skin, and sprinkle the ham with pepper before sending to the table.

To pickle pork

Mix together four and a half pounds of salt, a pound of brown sugar and one ounce of saltpeter, stirred into three gallons of water. Boil for half an hour, skimming every ten minutes. Set aside to cool, and when cold pour over the meat packed in a crock or keg.

Virginia recipe for curing ham

Put the ham into pickle made by putting into one and one-half gallons of water one-half pound of brown sugar, one-half ounce of saltpeter and two and one-quarter pounds of salt. Boil this mixture for half an hour, skimming frequently; then set aside to cool and pour over the ham. Leave for two weeks, remove the ham, wash it in fresh water; dip it, still wet, in bran, and coat thickly with it. Now take to the smokehouse and hang, hock end down, in smoke from hickory chips and sawdust for four weeks. Brush off the bran, wrap in brown paper and hang up until needed.

POULTRY

ROAST TURKEY

Draw, with care not to break the gall-bag. Wash out the cavity three times with cold water, adding a little soda to the second water. You can not be too careful in this part of your task.

Fill the body and craw with some one of the stuffings or "dressings" given below. Sew up the body and tie the skin covering the craw securely about the "scrag" or neck with cotton twine. Bind the legs and wings snugly to the body with cotton tape or strips of muslin. If the fowl be rather scrawny cover the breast with thin slices of fat salt pork. Put upon the grating of your covered roaster. Pour a cupful of boiling water over it to sear the skin and keep in the juices; cover and cook fifteen minutes to the pound, quite fast for twelve minutes or so, afterward steadily but slowly. Baste four times, each time very thoroughly, with the gravy from the pan.

A quarter of an hour before taking the turkey up, uncover and wash over with butter, then dredge with flour, and shut up in the oven to brown.

Make the gravy by stirring into the contents of the dripping-pan (when you have removed the turkey and are keeping it hot) the giblets, minced almost to powder, a tablespoonful of browned flour wet up with cold water, salt and pepper to taste. Skim before you add anything. Boil one minute and pour into a gravy-boat.

Always serve cranberry sauce with turkey, when you can get it.

Bread dressing for turkey

To a large cupful of crumbs allow a tablespoonful of minced fat pork. Season with pepper and, if you like, a little minced parsley. A little onion juice is an improvement. Moisten very slightly with cream, or milk.

Sausage dressing for turkey

Make as in last recipe, substituting sausage-meat for the pork. If partially cooked before it goes into the dressing, it is more wholesome.

Oyster stuffing for turkey

Make a stuffing for turkey in the ordinary way of dried breadcrumbs seasoned with parsley, thyme and sweet marjoram, and moistened with melted butter. To this add twenty small oysters chopped fine, and with this stuff the breast of the turkey.

Or to the ordinary seasoned bread-stuffing for a turkey add two dozen small oysters, moisten the crumbs slightly with the oyster liquor, and fill the breast of the turkey with the mixture.

Chestnut stuffing for turkey

Boil one quart of the large French or Italian chestnuts, shell and peel them. Mash smooth and rub into them two tablespoonfuls of butter, and salt and white pepper to taste. Stuff the turkey with this as you would any other kind of dressing.

Fillets of turkey with rice

Skin the breast of a plump turkey, and slice away the breast. Use a sharp knife and hold it almost horizontal while at work. The slices should be nearly half an inch thick, and as nearly uniform in size as possible. Dip in beaten egg, then in salted and peppered cracker-crumbs; again in the egg, and once more in the crumbs. Set on the ice while you cook the rice.

Put one cupful of clear chicken or turkey stock into a saucepan; add a cupful of rice, one-half teaspoonful of onion juice, and the same of salt, and simmer slowly until the liquid is ab sorbed. When the rice is tender add two tablespoonfuls of butter; one tablespoonful of grated cheese, and season to taste. Cover and let it stand at the side of the fire until the fillets are ready. Heat five or six spoonfuls of pure salad oil slowly in a frying-pan, and when it boils, cook the fillets in it to a nice brown. Mound the savory rice in the center of a hot dish and lay the fillets about it.

When properly made this is an elegant *entrée*.

Roast turkey, réchauffé

When but half of a large turkey has been cut away, the remainder can be made presentable for a second serving by "braising" it thus:

Cut very thin slices of fat salt pork and cover the untouched side with them, binding in place with soft twine. Lay the turkey, cut-side downward, in your covered roaster; pour a large cupful of weak stock or gravy under the grating, put on the lid and cook one hour, slowly, basting several times with the gravy in the pan below the roast. Take up the turkey, remove the pork, dredge with flour and set back in the oven, basting it with butter to "glaze" it as soon as the flour is wet through. Shut up to brown when you have drained away the gravy.

Strain this through a colander, thicken with browned flour, add half a can of minced champignons, cook two minutes, and pour into a boat.

Scallop of turkey and oysters

Cut cold roast or boiled turkey into inch-lengths, free from skin and gristle, and put a layer in the bottom of a buttered bake-dish. Season with salt and pepper, dot with butter and cover with minced raw oysters. Season this layer, scatter fine crumbs over it, put in more seasoned turkey, and go on in this order until your materials are used up. Pour in, then, a cupful of gravy made by boiling down bones and stuffing in a quart of water until reduced to one-third the original quantity of liquid, and straining out the bones. Cover with fine crumbs, dot with butter and bake, covered, forty-five minutes, then brown. You may omit the oysters, and have a plain turkey scallop.

Or substitute chopped mushrooms for the minced oysters.

Turkey and sausage pudding

This is a good way of using yesterday's turkey, if there is not a sightly half left to be set on again.

Into a buttered bake-dish put a layer of turkey, cut—not chopped—into half-inch lengths. Drop bits of butter over it, but no other seasoning. Cover with minced, cooked sausage-meat, and this with three or four olives chopped fine. Proceed in this way until the dish is ready for the crust. Pour in a cupful of rich gravy made of bones and stuffing; cover with a good biscuit-dough half an inch thick; cut a hole in the middle and bake, covered, three-quarters of an hour, then brown.

Ragout of turkey

Break the carcass of a roast turkey all to pieces, and chop what remnants of stuffing you have. Add a quart of cold water, and cook slowly until you have but a cupful of liquid. Strain and let it get cold. Skim off the fat, season with onion juice, kitchen bouquet, salt and paprika, and set over the fire with the turkey meat, cut into neat cubes, and a half cupful of champignons (or fresh mushrooms, if you have them). Bring quickly to a boil, thicken well with browned flour, boil up, add a glass of claret and serve. Lay sippets of fried bread around the ragout.

Boiled turkey

An undeniably tough turkey would be better boiled than roasted.

Clean, wash and fill with oyster-stuffing, for which a recipe was given a few pages back. Truss closely and sew up in a clean piece of white mosquito-netting. Lay in a pan and pour boiling water all over it from the tea-kettle, slowly, to toughen the skin and keep in the juices. Roll the turkey over and over in his hot bath, take out at the end of two minutes; put into a pot, cover deep with cold water, and heat gradually to a boil. Cook fifteen minutes to the pound, always gently. If the turkey be large and old, give him twenty minutes for each pound. Take the pot from the range, leave it covered for twenty minutes with the bird in it. Take him out, unwrap quickly, dish, wash freely with hot butter well-seasoned with salt and white pepper; pour a few spoonfuls of hot drawn butter over him, and serve. Send oyster sauce around with boiled turkey.

DUCKS

Roast ducks

Draw and clean, washing the inside in three waters, the second having a teaspoonful of baking-soda mixed with it.

Plunge into ice-cold water; leave them there for fifteen minutes; wipe well inside and out, and stuff with a forcemeat of dry crumbs seasoned with salt, pepper, onion juice and finely minced parsley.

Personally, I do not like sage in the stuffing. It gives a "medicated tang," to my way of thinking—or tasting. Many people, however, insist upon adding the venerable simple to the forcemeat. Do not moisten the stuffing. Put it in dry, packing well. Dredge the ducks with peppered and salted flour; lay upon the grating of your roaster, pour a cupful of boiling water over them, and roast, covered, from twelve to fifteen minutes to the pound, according to age. Baste four times with the gravy from the dripping-pan. Uncover, wash with butter, dredge with flour and brown.

To make the gravy, drain off the liquor from the pan; set in ice-water to throw up the grease, strain, add the giblets minced very fine, thicken with browned flour, and boil for two minutes.

POULTRY AND ENTREES
BRAISED SWEETBREADS
PAIR ROAST DUCKS
ROAST TURKEY
PAIR BOILED FOWLS GARNISHED WITH SLICED EGG
SCALLOPED CHICKEN

Serve with currant jelly, or apple sauce, and pass green peas with them.

Braised ducks

Young ducks are essential for this purpose. Lay three slices of fat corned ham upon the grating of your roaster, and upon them a minced onion, a stalk of celery, chopped, a sliced carrot and a tablespoonful of chopped parsley. Clean and truss, but do not stuff the ducks; lay them upon the prepared "bed," and pour a cupful of boiling water over them. Cover the pan and let them cook, closely covered, in a moderate oven for about two hours. Take up the ducks, strain the liquor from the pan, and let it cool enough to remove all the fat. Then put it into a saucepan, and let it boil. Add one teaspoonful of lemon juice, and thicken it slightly with browned flour. Return the fowls to the sauce till hot again, then serve with the sauce poured over them.

Creole salmi of duck

Melt in a saucepan two tablespoonfuls of butter, and stir into this a half tablespoonful, each, of chopped ham, onion, celery, sweet pepper and parsley, with a tablespoonful of flour, a quarter of a teaspoonful of salt, and a half teaspoonful of paprika. Stir for three minutes, then add a cupful of consommé, two cloves and a blade of mace. Simmer for an hour; strain and add to it two cupfuls of cold duck, cut into neat pieces an inch long. Boil one minute to heat the meat thoroughly, and serve.

Garnish with sippets of fried bread.

CHICKENS

Roast chickens

Singe to get rid of down, draw and wash well, rinsing the cavity of each fowl with soda and water. Wipe and fill bodies and craws with a stuffing of dry crumbs, well-seasoned with pepper, salt and butter. Tie up the neck and bind legs and wings close to the body with soft cord or tapes.

Lay upon the grating of your covered roaster; dash a cupful of boiling water over them, cover, and roast fifteen minutes to the pound. Drain off the gravy, and set in iced water to throw up the fat. Wash the chickens over with butter, dredge with flour and brown. Clip the threads and dish. Thicken the gravy with browned flour, add the chopped giblets (previously boiled tender), boil up once and turn into a boat.

Boiled fowls

Prepare as for roasting; sew up in white netting, or in coarse lace, and souse four times in boiling water. Then put over the fire in cold, slightly salted water, covering deeply; bring slowly to the boil, and cook gently fifteen minutes to the pound.

Have ready egg-or oyster-sauce, or bread-sauce. Pour a few spoonfuls of hot butter, salted and peppered, over the chickens, the rest into a boat.

Smothered chickens

Broilers, and other really young fowls, are necessary for this dish. Split down the back when you have cleaned and washed them. Lay them out flat on the grating of your roaster, skin side down, and put into a very hot oven, covered. Have ready half a cupful of melted butter, and after five minutes baste the chickens well with this. Turn them as soon as the inside has colored slightly; baste again with butter; when nearly done dredge thickly with flour and wash again with butter. When they are brown, and the flesh is tender in the joints, they are done. Thirty minutes should be sufficient. Baste frequently, and as soon as they are browned you may add a little hot water to the butter.

Take up the chickens and keep them hot, thicken the gravy with browned flour, and boil one minute before pouring into a boat.

If the chickens are large, make a gash at each joint before cooking, and cook longer. This is sometimes called "baked broiled chicken," sometimes, "chicken broiled in the oven."

Broiled chicken

When you have cleaned and washed the young chickens, split down the back, so as to leave the breast in one piece. Lay in lemon juice and salad oil for half an hour, wipe lightly, pepper and salt, and lay within a well-greased broiler, skin side uppermost. Broil ten or twelve minutes to the pound, according to age and weight, turning often and never allowing it to drip upon the coals. When done, lay, breast upward, upon a hot dish, rub all over with a mixture of butter, lemon juice and minced parsley, and serve.

Pass fried potatoes with it.

Baked fried chicken

Here again you must have young chickens. Clean, wash and cut up at every joint, dividing the breast into two pieces. Lay in a marinade of salad oil and lemon juice for half an hour; drain, but do not wipe. Roll in beaten egg, then in cracker-crumbs. Repeat the process and leave on the ice for an hour. Lay, then, upon the grating of your roaster, pour a little gravy in the pan beneath, and cover closely. At the end of twenty minutes, baste with melted butter, carefully, not to disturb the crumb coating; re-cover, and at the end of half an hour more, baste plentifully with the gravy. Now let them brown. Send bread-sauce in with them, and garnish with parsley.

Braised chicken

Cover the grating of your roaster with a blanket of vegetables; a carrot, a small young turnip, an onion, a young carrot, a stalk of celery, all cut up small; a little chopped parsley, and two tablespoonfuls of finely minced salt pork. Have ready the chicken, cleaned and trussed, but not stuffed. Lay, breast upward, on the vegetables and pork. Pour a little boiling water over him from the teakettle, and set, covered, in the oven. Cover closely and cook at least twenty minutes to the pound if the chicken be young. If old, extend the time. At the end of one hour lift the cover and baste with butter, then with the water from the pan, and shut up for an hour longer. Uncover then, rub with butter, dredge with flour and brown.

Drain the gravy with the vegetables from the pan, rub through a colander into a saucepan, thicken with browned flour, boil up and serve in a boat.

Baked chicken

Clean as usual, and cover with thin slices of cold boiled ham. Corned ham is better than smoked, but either will do. Wind fine cotton cord around and around the ham to hold it in place; lay upon the grating of your roaster; pour over it a cup of boiling hot stock, scatter parsley and sprinkle onion juice upon it; cover closely to keep in the steam and cook slowly twenty-five minutes to the pound. Baste three times within the first hour. Test with a skewer or a fork. If tender, it should be unwrapped, basted with butter, dredged with flour and left uncovered to brown.

Garnish with the ham cut into strips. Thicken the gravy with browned flour, season and cook one minute.

Fricasseed chicken

Clean as usual, and dissect so thoroughly that the carver will have nothing for his knife to do in "helping" the dish. The breast and the back should be in two pieces, each, and every joint be separate from the next.

Wash, but do not wipe. Arrange the pieces, dripping wet, in a pot, scatter over each layer minced onion, parsley and chopped fat pork; season with salt and pepper. Cover the pot very closely and set it where it will not begin to boil under an hour. Increase the heat somewhat, but cook slowly throughout. *Cook until done!* The toughest tendons will yield to slow stewing in time.

When assured that your end is gained, take out the meat with a split spoon, heap upon a platter, the white at one end, the dark at the other, and keep hot while making the gravy. To do this, pour into a bowl, set in iced water to make the fat rise. Skim, return to the pot and add a cupful of hot milk thickened with a tablespoonful of butter rubbed into one of flour. Boil one minute—when you have added a pinch of soda. Have ready two well beaten eggs, add the boiling gravy gradually and pour over the chicken.

This is an old family recipe and warranted excellent.

Pass boiled rice with this dish.

A brown fricassee

Prepare as for ordinary fricassee. Fry half a pound of fat salt pork, sliced thin, in a pan; when they hiss and smoke, put in a large sliced onion and cook until it colors. Now dredge the pieces of chicken with flour and fry, a few pieces at a time, in the same fat, turning several times. When they begin to brown turn all into a pot with the shreds of pork and onion. Add a very small cupful of stock; cover closely and cook until done.

Have ready a brown roux, made by cooking together a great spoonful of butter with the same of browned flour. Stir in a teaspoonful of kitchen bouquet, and add to the gravy left in the pot after the chicken is dished. Cook two minutes and pour over the dished chicken. Set in the oven for three minutes before serving.

A pilau of chicken

Joint a tender broiler and leave for half an hour in a bath of salad oil and lemon juice. Drain, without wiping. Have ready three tablespoonfuls of butter, hissing hot, in a frying-pan. Fry a sliced onion in it, and then put in the chicken. Cook for ten minutes, turning often, and empty the contents of the pan into a pot with a broad bottom. Pour upon them a cupful of strained tomato sauce, and the same of weak stock—chicken or veal. Stew gently until the chicken is tender; take it up and keep in a hot colander set in the oven and covered closely. Drain off every drop of gravy, return to the fire and add three-quarters of a cupful of rice which has soaked for an hour in cold water. Cook fast until the rice is soft but not broken. Put the chicken back into the pot, mixing well with the rice, simmer three minutes and heap upon a heated platter. Sift Parmesan cheese thickly over all.

Boiled chicken stuffed with oysters

Prepare as usual for boiling or roasting, then fill body and craw with small oysters, which have been dipped in peppered and salted melted butter. Sew up in netting and boil twenty minutes to the pound if young, thirty minutes if old. Unwrap, wash over with butter and lemon juice; pour a few spoonfuls of oyster sauce upon them, the rest into a boat.

Chicken en casserole

Truss the chicken, which must be young and plump, as for roasting. Into a frying-pan on top of the range put two tablespoonfuls of butter, a sliced onion and carrot, a bay leaf and a sprig of thyme. When the vegetables are slightly browned put, with the chicken, into the casserole, add a pint of well-seasoned stock, cover the casserole and cook in the oven for three-quarters of an hour. After it has been in the oven for this length of time, drop in a dozen potato balls, or strips that have been cut from raw potatoes and sauté in hot butter, and a dozen French mushrooms. Season the gravy to taste, and leave the casserole uncovered that the chicken may brown. Ten minutes before taking from the oven, pour over the chicken two tablespoonfuls of sherry. When you take the chicken from the oven sprinkle it with minced parsley. Serve in the casserole.

Creamed stewed chicken

Cut up a fowl as for fricassee, and put over the fire in enough cold water to cover it well. Bring gradually to a gentle boil. When it begins to bubble, add a stalk of celery, some chopped parsley and two tablespoonfuls of minced onion, with a bay leaf. Simmer until tender before seasoning with salt and pepper.

Make a white roux in a frying-pan of two tablespoonfuls of but ter cooked with the same quantity of flour. As soon as they are well mixed, stir into them, a teaspoonful at a time, a large cupful of strained and skimmed gravy from the pot. Have ready half a cup of cream, heated, with a pinch of soda. Add this to the thickened gravy also, very slowly, not to curdle the cream. Do not boil after the cream goes in. Arrange the chicken upon a broad platter; pour the creamed gravy over it, and garnish with dumplings cooked in the gravy left in the large pot, after the reserved cupful and the chicken are taken out.

Dumplings for chicken stew

Into a pint of flour sift a heaping teaspoonful of baking-powder, and a quarter-teaspoonful of salt, and sift the flour twice. Now rub in a tablespoonful of shortening and wet with enough milk to make a dough that can be rolled out. Roll and cut into rounds, and drop these into the boiling gravy. They should be done in ten minutes.

Mexican hot tamales (No. 1)

Boil a fowl until tender; salt while boiling. Chop very fine and season with plenty of cayenne pepper and a little garlic. Have ready a thick paste made of one cupful of corn-meal mixed with a little boiling water. Shape the meat into rolls the size of the little finger, and encase each in the corn-meal paste. Take the inner husks of Indian corn, cut off the ends, leaving the husks about six inches long, and wash them in boiling water.

Wrap each tamale in a corn husk; throw two or three Mexican peppers into the liquor in which the chicken was boiled, and cook the tamales in it for fifteen minutes.

Mexican hot tamales (No. 2)

Boil a fowl until tender; strip the meat from the bones and chop fine. Mince half a pound of seeded raisins, and a half-cupful of stoned olives, with one young red pepper chopped "exceeding fine." Mix all well together, and stir to a paste with two cupfuls of Indian meal; wet with scalding water, season with salt, onion juice and a teaspoonful of sugar. Add more boiling water until you can stir over the fire for fifteen or twenty minutes. Then add six hard-boiled eggs minced fine; meantime lay smooth the soft inner husks of green corn, and tear some into strips for tying; lay upon two of the husks as much of the paste mixture as they will contain, wrap them about it and tie each roll with the stripped husk; drop these rolls into boiling salted water, and boil them for one hour.

If well seasoned, these are very savory.

Chop suey

(A Chinese recipe)

One-half chicken (or quarter chicken and as much fresh pork, or you can make it all pork, but chicken is much better), one large onion, a handful of mushrooms, a stalk of celery, six Chinese potatoes, a bowl of rice, a small dessert dish of Chinese sauce (which answers for salt).

When the chicken is cleaned scrape the meat from the bones and cut into strips about one and a half inches long and one-half inch wide. If pork is used, cut the strips the same length. Slice the onions thin; soak the mushrooms ten minutes in water, then remove the stems; cut the celery into pieces one and a half inches long. Chinese potatoes require no cooking; simply wash and slice.

First put chicken (or chicken and pork, or pork) into a frying-pan with fat and fry until done, but not brown or hard. Then add the sliced onions and cook a little. Add mushrooms. Now pour enough sauce over the ingredients to make them brown. Then add some water and stew a few minutes. Add celery, and after a minute add the potatoes. Finally, add a little floured water to it, making gravy of the water which stewed it.

The Chinese potatoes, mushrooms and Chinese sauce can be procured at any Chinese grocery. If the rice is not cooked properly it will detract greatly from the good taste of the chop suey. Otherwise it is a very palatable dish.

To those who do not know how to serve it I will say: Put some rice into a bowl, then add as much chop suey as you want. Mix and pour in enough of the sauce that was used in cooking it. Tea is usually taken with this dish.

Canned chicken

Joint the chicken as for fricassee, cover with cold water, and bring slowly to the boil. Simmer until tender, but not broken. When done add salt to the liquor, boil all up once, then remove the chicken and pack in wide-mouthed jars. Pack in as tightly as possible. Stand the jars at the side of the range in a pan of boiling water, boil up the chicken liquor, fill the jars to overflowing with the scalding liquid and seal immediately.

GEESE

Roast goose

Draw, clean, singe and truss as you would prepare a turkey. Always put onion and a suspicion of sage in the stuffing. Lay upon the grating of your roaster; pour a cup of boiling water over him to cicatrice the skin and keep in the juices, and roast, covered, twenty minutes to the pound if of reasonable age. If of unreasonable, cook slowly, basting often with the liquor in the dripping-pan, at least half an hour for each obdurate pound. A goose is a most uncertain quantity.

At the last, wash with butter, pepper and salt him, and dredge with flour, then brown. Drain off and skim the fat from the gravy before you season the goose. Goose-grease is valuable in the domestic pharmacopœia, but neither palatable nor wholesome.

Thicken the gravy with browned flour, add the giblets minced very fine, boil up and it is ready.

Serve apple sauce with him.

Braised goslings

Clean and truss without stuffing. Prepare a bed for them by slicing a carrot, an onion, a turnip (all younglings, like the birds), also a pared apple, and cutting a stalk of celery into bits. With these cover the grating of your roaster; lay the birds upon them, dredge with salt, pepper and a little powdered sage, when you have poured a little boiling water over them from the kettle. Cover, and roast slowly fifteen minutes to the pound. Wash with butter, dredge with flour and brown.

Take the goslings up and keep hot while you make the gravy. Rub vegetables and liquor through a colander into a bowl. Set this in cold water to throw up the grease. Skim, thicken with browned flour, adding two teaspoonfuls of tomato catsup, boil up and serve.

Serve apple sauce and green peas, or Lima beans, with the goslings which are most eatable when half-grown.

Salmi of goose

Cut the remains of a roast goose into small pieces, about an inch long and half as wide. Have ready a gravy made by boiling down the bones and toughest scraps until you have a cupful of strong stock. Add to this a carrot, a young turnip, a tomato, an apple and a stalk of celery, all cut into dice, and the vegetables parboiled for ten minutes. Simmer in the gravy until you can run them through your vegetable press. Put in the meat and cook slowly until tender. Thicken with browned flour.

GAME

The lower one descends in the social scale the less appreciation is there of game of any variety. What the plebeian terms "wild things" play a small part upon his menu—indeed, are probably altogether absent from it. He turns with a shrug from jugged hare, broiled quail and roast partridge to feast upon what is known in his set as "plain roast and boiled." It is the epicure and the man of refined and cultivated gastronomic tastes who can appreciate good game.

Just here it may be well to remark that game need not of necessity be "high." Some persons profess to prefer it when it has been kept so long as to be a little offensive to the olfactory organs. Whether or not this be affectation is not for us to judge. Suffice it to say that the following recipes are for the preparation of well-seasoned game, and not for viands that bear a distressing resemblance to carrion.

Saddle of venison

Rub the meat thoroughly with melted butter, and wrap it in buttered paper. Put into a covered roaster with a little water in the bottom of the pan. Allow at least twenty minutes' roasting to every pound of meat. Half an hour before the meat is done remove the cover and the paper, and cook, basting every ten minutes with butter and a little melted currant jelly. At the end of the half-hour transfer the venison to a hot platter; strain the drippings left in the pan, add to them a cupful of boiling water, a dash of nut meg, salt, pepper, two tablespoonfuls of butter and the same quantity of currant jelly. When the butter and the jelly are melted, pour the sauce into a gravy-boat and send to the table with the venison.

The loin, the haunch and the leg of venison may be cooked in like manner, and may be served with propriety even at a "company dinner," although the saddle, like Abou Ben Adhem's name, "leads all the rest."

Venison steak

It requires about three minutes more time to broil than beefsteak, even when tender. If doubtful, lay in olive oil and lemon juice for two hours before cooking. Drain without wiping, and broil over clear hot coals, turning often to avoid scorching.

Take up, lay upon a very hot dish, sprinkle with salt and paprika and spread on both sides a mixture of butter stirred up with currant jelly. Cover and leave over hot water five minutes before it goes to table.

Roast partridges

Select plump birds, pick and clean as you would chickens, washing them out quickly in cold water. To allow them to lie in the water injures their flavor. Tie the legs and wings closely to the sides and put the birds in a covered roaster with a cup of water under them. Rub with butter, dredge with flour and cook for half an hour. Now remove the cover of the roaster and baste the birds plentifully with melted butter. Replace the cover, cook for fifteen minutes longer, uncover and brown.

Woodcock

May be roasted according to the foregoing recipe, but as it is a smaller bird than the partridge, less time will be required in the cooking. The fashionable way of cooking woodcock is what is known as "with the trail." To prepare the woodcock, wash them and remove the crops. Fold the legs and wings close to the body and bend the head forward so that the long bill may be run, skewer-wise, through the legs and wings, thus holding them in place. Put two slices of toast in the bottom of a large, deep fireproof soup-plate, and place two birds, side by side, upon this; put a lump of butter upon each, and invert a large saucer or small plate over them. Over the opening left about the edge of the saucer lay a strip of pastry, that all air may be excluded. Set in the oven for seven minutes, then make an incision in the pastry and allow the steam to escape. Cover this small hole with a bit of fresh pastry, return the birds to the oven and cook for half an hour. Pour melted butter over the woodcock, serve on the toast on which they were cooked, and garnish with strips of the browned pastry.

GAME
ROAST WOODCOCK
ROAST BELGIAN HARE
QUAIL ON TOAST
ROAST VENISON
ROAST PARTRIDGE

As some persons do not like the "trail," it may be well to remark that drawn woodcock may be cooked according to this recipe.

Broiled quail

Pick and draw the birds, and remove the heads and feet. Wipe out the bodies with a wet cloth, split down the back and lay open upon a gridiron. Broil on both sides, taking care that the delicate flesh is not dried into tastelessness. Lay the quail upon slices of buttered toast, put a lump of butter upon each, and sprinkle with butter and salt. Set in the oven until the butter melts, then send to the table.

Roasted quail

Clean and wash in two waters. The second should have a teaspoonful of baking-soda dissolved in it. Rinse with clear water and wipe the inside of each bird with a soft linen cloth. Put within the body of each a single fine oyster, bind legs and wings down with fine soft cotton. Have ready thin slices of fat salt pork, two for each bird. Cover the breasts with these, binding with soft string; lay upon the grating of the roaster, pour a little boiling water from the kettle upon each, and roast from twenty to twenty-five minutes. Five minutes before you take them up, remove the pork, wash with butter, dredge with flour and brown.

Cut rounds of stale bread, toast and butter them; soak with gravy from the pan, and lay a bird upon each.

You may omit the oysters and fill the birds instead with a forcemeat of seasoned crumbs. Chopped oysters also make a good stuffing, while some prefer to roast them uncovered and without the pork covering.

RABBITS AND HARES

In America "hare" and "rabbit" are interchangeable terms. The wild rabbit of the Middle States and New England is the "old hare" of the South, and one with the "Br'er Rabbit" of negro folk-lore. Hence I shall use the names indifferently in the recipes dealing with the wily *coureur du bois* of both regions.

Barbecued rabbit

Wash the cleaned and beheaded rabbit thoroughly, and cut it open all along the under side of the body. Make deep incisions across the backbone that the heat may penetrate to the center of the flesh. Spread the hare open on a gridiron and broil, turning frequently. When done, transfer to a hot platter, rub with butter, cover and keep warm in the oven while you make the sauce that is to accompany the game.

In a small saucepan melt three tablespoonfuls of butter, and stir into it two tablespoonfuls of vinegar, a teaspoonful of French mustard and a teaspoonful of minced parsley. When very hot pour this sauce over the rabbit. Let it stand covered in a hot dish five minutes before serving.

Roast rabbit

Leave the heads on in cleaning them. Stuff the bodies with a forcemeat of fat salt pork, minced onion and fine crumbs, well seasoned with pepper and salt. Sew them up with fine thread and lay upon thin slices of pork covering the grating of the roaster. Lay other slices of pork over them, pour over all a cupful of stock and roast one hour. Remove the pork then, wash with butter, dredge with flour and brown.

Drain off the gravy, lay the bits of bacon about the rabbit in the dish; thicken the gravy with browned floor. Boil up, add a tablespoonful of tomato catsup and a glass of claret, and take from the fire.

Casserole of rabbit

Skin, clean and cut up as for fricassee. Make two pieces of each back. Fry a dozen slices of fat salt pork in a frying-pan, then two sliced onions to a pale brown. Strain the fat back into the pan, keeping the shreds of onion and pork in a bowl by themselves. Pepper, salt and dredge with flour the jointed hare and fry, a few pieces at a time, in the same fat. Have ready parboiled about two dozen potato balls and half as many baby onions, with half a cupful of button mushrooms, canned or fresh. When the meat is well seared on both sides, lay some in the casserole, then six potato balls and two or three onions with a few mushrooms. Strew the chopped salt pork over them, season with pepper and dredge with browned flour. Proceed in this order until the casserole is full. Cover with cold stock or gravy, put on the cover, filling in the cracks where it joins the casserole with flour paste; and cook slowly three hours before opening it. If tender, then drain off the gravy carefully not to disturb the various layers. Put into a saucepan, thicken with browned flour; season with tomato catsup and salt and pepper if needed. Boil one minute; stir in a tablespoonful of tart jelly and the same of lemon juice; return to the casserole; replace the cover and leave in an open oven for five minutes before serving.

Stewed rabbits

Clean and joint as for the casserole, cutting each joint and halving the backs. Proceed in the same way, also, to fry the pork, onion and meat when you have peppered, salted and floured this last.

Then pack in a saucepan, pour in enough stock (or butter and water) barely to cover it; season with salt, pepper, sweet herbs and onion juice; cover closely and stew slowly for two hours, or until tender. Drain the gravy into another saucepan, setting that containing the meat, covered, in a larger vessel of boiling water. Thicken the gravy with a big lump of butter worked up with browned flour, a teaspoonful of Worcestershire sauce and one of kitchen bouquet; pour back upon the meat and let all stand together in boiling water for five minutes.

Belgian hares

May be cooked in any of the ways described in recipes for preparing wild hares for table use.

Wild turkey

Clean and truss as you would a tame turkey, but wet the stuffing with melted butter, and while roasting the bird must be basted freely with butter. Six or seven times are not too much. The flesh, while sweet and peculiarly "gamy," is drier than that of his domesticated brother.

As it is impossible to determine his age before shooting him, there are even chances that he will be tougher than if fattened for the table. Should this prove to be the case, steam him over boiling water for an hour before putting him into the roaster.

Send currant or grape jelly around with him instead of cranberry, and add a little lemon juice to the thickened gravy. Garnish him with "link" sausages, boiled and then fried.

Roast grouse

Here again we have dry birds. Clean, rinse out well with soda and water, then with pure water; wipe inside and out, and cover with thin slices of corned ham—more fat than lean. Bind criss-cross with soft twine or narrow tape, pour a cup of boiling water over them, and roast forty minutes, basting with the gravy in the pan three times. Take off the bacon, wash the birds with butter, dredge with flour and brown while you make the gravy.

Thicken this with browned flour, add the juice of half a lemon, boil up, pour in a small glass of claret and serve. Garnish with the ham and whole olives.

Braised wild pigeons

Clean, wash carefully; put an olive in the body of each and bind legs and wings neatly to the sides of the birds.

Fry six or eight slices of fat salt pork in the frying-pan until crisp, but not burned. Strain the fat back, lay in the pigeons and roll over and over in the boiling grease until seared on all sides. Take them up and keep hot. Add a spoonful of butter to the hot fat, and when it hisses, fry a large onion, sliced, in it. Lay the pigeons upon the grating of the roaster, pour the boiling fat and onion over them; add a cupful of weak stock; cover closely and cook steadily for three-quarters of an hour. Test the birds with a skewer or fork, and if tender wash with butter, dredge and brown. Remove to a hot dish and make the gravy.

Thicken with a brown roux, and season to taste; stir in a dozen stoned olives. "Pimolas" are nice if you can get them. If you can get fresh mushrooms, fry or broil a dozen and lay about the pigeons when they are dished.

Pass currant jelly with them.

Stewed wild pigeons

Wash well, when you have cleaned them, rinsing out with soda and water, and leave in salt and water for an hour. Chop fat corned pork fine, season with onion juice and paprika, and put a teaspoonful into the body of each bird. Truss neatly, winding the body about with soft thread, and put into a saucepan. Cover with cold water and simmer gently until tender. Take up then and lay in a fire-proof dish. Wash with butter beaten to a cream with lemon juice, onion juice and finely minced parsley. Cover and set in the oven over hot water.

Thicken the gravy with browned flour, beat in a great spoonful of currant jelly, add two dozen champignons cut into halves, boil one minute, return the pigeons to the gravy and simmer ten minutes.

SQUIRRELS

The large gray squirrel of the Southern and Middle States is reckoned by many epicures as superior to rabbits or hares in richness and delicacy of flavor. The small red roisterer who chatters in groves and coppice, and devours the eggs and young of songbirds, is secured from trapper and gunner by his worthlessness as an article of food. There is so little of him and that little is so juiceless that powder and shot would be wasted upon him.

His gray cousin-german is so toothsome when properly cooked, one wonders that there are not preserves of them near all our large towns. They are easily raised, hardy and, with little care, multiply rapidly.

Broiled squirrels

Skin, clean and lay in a marinade of salad oil and lemon juice for one hour. Drain, but do not wipe. Lay upon a gridiron, wide open, ribs downward. Broil over clear coals, turning as they begin to drip. When done, remove to a hot water dish, wash with butter creamed with lemon juice and seasoned with pepper and salt. Cover and let them stand five minutes before serving.

Stewed squirrels

Clean, lay in salt and water half an hour, then joint, cutting the back into two pieces. Put into a saucepan, sprinkle with minced onion, and cover with cold water. Cover closely and stew one hour before adding four tablespoonfuls of fat salt pork minced fine. Cook for another hour, or until tender. Take up the squirrels and keep hot. Stir into the gravy a great spoonful of butter rolled in flour. Have ready in another vessel half a cupful of cream, heated with a pinch of soda, into which has been beaten a raw egg. Pour the gravy over the squirrels, simmer one minute, add the cream and take at once from the fire.

Roast squirrels

Clean, wash and lay for one hour in salad oil and lemon juice. Have ready a large cupful of bread-crumbs soaked in enough cream to moisten them, add a cupful of minced mushrooms and pepper, salt and onion juice to your taste. Fill the animals with this stuffing, sew up and truss, rub all over with butter, lay in a baking-dish and nearly cover with weak stock. When done, make a piquante sauce from the gravy in the pan by adding the juice of half a lemon, a teaspoonful of Worcestershire sauce, paprika and salt to taste. Boil up and pour into a boat.

Virginia stew of squirrels

Clean, wash and joint three squirrels. Lay in salt and water for half an hour. Put then into a broad pot in this order: First, a layer of chopped fat salt pork, then one of minced onions; next, of parboiled potatoes, sliced thin; then follow successive layers of green corn cut from the cob, Lima beans and the squirrels. Proceed in this order, seasoning each layer with black, and more lightly, with cayenne pepper, until all the materials are used up. Cover with four quarts of boiling water, and put a tight lid on the pot. Stew gently for three hours before adding a quart of tomatoes, peeled and cut into bits, two teaspoonfuls of white sugar and a tablespoonful of salt. Cook an hour more; stir in four tablespoonfuls of butter, cut up in two of flour, boil three minutes and turn into a tureen.

This is the genuine recipe, over a century old, for making the far-famed "Brunswick stew" eaten in perfection at Old Virginia races, "barbecues" and political dinners.

Chickens, lamb and veal may be used in place of squirrels, also "old hares."

Barbecued squirrels

Broil, as already directed, lay upon a hot dish, ribs downward, and cover with a sauce made by heating together four tablespoonfuls of vinegar with two of butter; a teaspoonful, each, of sugar and made mustard, a half teaspoonful, each, of salt and pepper. Boil one minute; pour over the squirrels, and let them stand, covered, ten minutes before serving.

GAME PIES

Squirrel pie

Clean and joint the squirrels, cutting the backs into three pieces, each. Put six slices of fat salt pork into a saucepan, fry three minutes, then put in the squirrels and fry to a light brown in this fat, adding, as the meat begins to yellow, a chopped onion, some chopped parsley and a cupful of mushrooms; sprinkle over them two tablespoonfuls of flour; add a pint of stock and simmer slowly until the meat is tender, seasoning, at the last, with salt and pepper. Boil one minute; pour over the squirrels, and let them cool before putting into bakedish; pour in a gravy formed by stewing, add a few more mushrooms and a couple of hard-boiled eggs cut in slices; cover with a good crust and bake one hour.

Rabbit pie

Clean, wash and joint, cutting each back into three pieces. Leave in salt and water for half an hour; wipe, and rub well with lemon juice, salt and pepper; where the meat is thick, make several cuts with a knife that the seasoning may penetrate. Lay them in a saucepan, add cold water to cover, then put in a bay-leaf, eight peppercorns, a bit of mace and two sliced onions. Cook slowly till the meat is tender. Have ready a buttered bakedish and when the meat is cool lay within this, alternately with sliced boiled eggs, a few minced olives and a dozen tiny young onions which have been parboiled. Thicken with browned flour the liquor in which the rabbit was stewed, and add more salt if needed. Strain it over the meat, using enough to make it quite moist. Cover the dish with a rich pastry or baking-powder crust, make a wide cut in the center, and bake, covered, half an hour, then brown.

Squirrel or rabbit pot-pie

Proceed as with the preceding recipes, until you are ready to pack in the dish. Add, then, three potatoes parboiled and sliced, and tiny dumplings, like marbles, made of a good biscuit dough; cut round and boil ten minutes in the gravy before this goes into the pie.

Pie of small birds

I wish I could preface the recipe with the information that English sparrows are available for this purpose. If not suppressed they are likely to lessen the supply of edible small birds and of warblers of all kinds to a degree inconceivable by those who have not watched their achievements in this line.

Blackbirds, ricebirds and snipe may be used in families or as neighbors in the manufacture of our dish.

Clean and stew the birds for half-an-hour in weak stock. Let them get perfectly cold in this gravy; take out, put an oyster in the body of each. Arrange around the inside of your bake-dish, the necks all against the rim, the tails pointing toward the center. Put a bit of butter upon each breast and sprinkle very finely minced salt pork over all. Thicken the gravy with browned flour, season well and pour upon the birds. Cover with a good crust, cut a slit in the middle, and bake, covered, half-an-hour. Then brown.

Quail pie

Joint as you would a chicken for fricassee, cover the baking-dish bottom with thin slices of streaky bacon, first partially boiled to extract the salt; cover with a good white sauce, a few mushrooms, or a little mushroom catsup, and some chopped parsley, then with puff-paste. Cut a slit in the middle; bake, covered, and slowly, one hour. Uncover and brown.

A combination game pie

Wild pigeons and quails, ricebirds, snipe, woodcock—in fact, any small edible birds—may be blended in this. Clean the birds and, if tough, stew them in weak stock. If they are large—that is, too large for a whole bird to be served for one portion—cut them in halves through the breastbone. If the birds are young and tender they may be browned in hot butter; first dredging them with flour, instead of parboiling. Arrange them in a deep, round baking-dish with the breasts up and the feet all pointing toward the center.

Make a gravy of the stock in which they were parboiled, season well with salt, pepper, onion juice and the juice of half a lemon; thicken with a roux of butter and browned flour. Fill in the central space left by the feet of the game with mushrooms, a cupful of small drained oysters, two kidneys, cut into quarters, half a cupful of pimolas, or with plain olives, stoned, and three hard-boiled eggs minced fine with one dozen button onions, parboiled. Pour the rich gravy over all. Cover with a good puff-paste; make a slit in the middle and bake, covered, half-an-hour, then brown.

Pigeon pie

Clean and joint the pigeons and wipe each piece with a damp cloth. Sprinkle with pepper and salt, and sauté in shallow dripping in which an onion has first been fried. Grease a pudding dish and put a layer of the fried pigeons in the bottom; cover this with minced salt pork, sliced hard-boiled eggs, and the minced pigeon giblets. Each piece of pigeon should have been rolled in browned flour before going into the dish. Arrange the layers as directed, until the dish is full—having the top layer of the minced salt pork. Pour a cupful of good stock over all; cover the pie with puff-paste; cut a slit in this to allow the steam to escape, and bake in a steady oven for an hour.

Venison pie

Stew gently until tender some small pieces of fresh venison, and some slices of sweet potato; season with salt and pepper. Put into a baking-dish and cover with a paste made from the drippings from a roast of venison, allowing one-half pound of fat to one pound of flour.

DINNER VEGETABLES

THE ARISTOCRATIC ASPARAGUS

A writer upon dietetics says—whether truthfully or not each of us can judge for himself—"Asparagus has nothing plebeian about it, as has the onion, the potato, the cabbage, turnip or parsnip. It is essentially a gentleman's vegetable, and is an aristocrat from tip to stalk."

It is becoming more and more customary to serve certain vegetables as a course by themselves, instead of with the meat and its attendant vegetables, as in days gone by. The housekeeper, who is often sorely perplexed as to what *entrée* she shall serve with a dinner, eagerly welcomes this custom. Asparagus, artichokes and cauliflower may be sent in as separate courses.

Boiled asparagus

Cut off the tough lower part of your asparagus-stalks and save them to stew for flavoring your next soup. Lay the asparagus in cold water for fifteen minutes, then tie carefully into a bundle with a piece of soft string. Put into a saucepan large enough for them to lie at full length. Cover with salted, boiling water and boil until tender. If young, twenty minutes should suffice. Drain carefully and lay neatly on a hot dish. Pass drawn butter with the asparagus.

Asparagus on toast

Cut the woody part from a bunch of asparagus, and with a soft piece of twine tie it into a loose bundle. Have ready, boiling, enough salted water to cover the asparagus. The saucepan con taining this should be large enough to allow the asparagus to lie at full length. Boil until tender, but not until the green tips begin to break. Spread upon a platter crustless slices of buttered toast; drain the asparagus, and lay it in a neat pile upon the toast. Of course the string must be removed from the bundle. Just before sending to the table pour a white sauce over the asparagus. An excellent plan is to pour this sauce only over the green ends of the stalks, leaving the white ends uncovered, that the fingers need not be soiled in handling the vegetable.

Baked asparagus

Cut the tender halves of the asparagus-stalks into inch-lengths. Cook for fifteen minutes in salted boiling water, then drain. Grease a pudding dish and put in the bottom a layer of the asparagus. Sprinkle this with fine bread-crumbs, bits of butter, pepper and salt and small pieces of hard-boiled egg. Now put in another layer of asparagus, more crumbs, etc., and so on until the dish is full. The last layer must be sprinkled with crumbs and bits of butter. Bake for half an hour, and serve in the dish in which it is cooked.

Asparagus tips cachés

Cut the tops from square breakfast-rolls, and scoop the crumbs from the insides, leaving box-like crusts. Butter the outside and inside of these hollowed rolls and set them with the tops beside them in the oven to dry and brown lightly.

Boil asparagus tips tender in salted water and drain. Have ready on the stove a white sauce made by cooking together a tablespoonful of butter and one of flour, and adding to them a cup and a half of milk. Stir into this sauce the asparagus tips, and pepper and salt to taste. Fill the hollowed rolls with the mixture, replace the tops and set in the oven just long enough to become very hot.

Creamed asparagus

Reject the lower halves of your asparagus stalks and boil the upper halves until they are very tender. Then drain and chop. Cook together a tablespoonful of butter and two of flour until they bubble, pour on them a pint of milk with a bit of soda dissolved in it. Stir until smooth and of the consistency of cream, add the minced asparagus, with salt and pepper to taste. Set this mixture aside until cool, then beat into it three well-whipped eggs and two tablespoonfuls of cream. Pour into a greased pudding dish and bake covered for twenty minutes; uncover and brown.

Asparagus á la vinaigrette (No. 1)

Boil the asparagus according to the directions given in the preceding recipe. When done, drain and set aside until cold, then place in the ice-box until wanted. Lay upon a chilled platter and pour over the stalks the following dressing:

Put three tablespoonfuls of salad oil into a bowl and stir into it a tablespoonful of vinegar, a saltspoonful, each, of salt and sugar, and a dash of paprika.

The asparagus and the dressing that accompany it should be served very cold.

Asparagus á la vinaigrette (No. 2)

Cook as directed in recipe for boiled asparagus. While the vegetable is cooking make a hot French dressing by putting together in a saucepan over the fire half-a-dozen tablespoonfuls of salad oil, two of vinegar, two teaspoonfuls of French mustard, half a teaspoonful of sugar, salt and pepper to taste. When the asparagus is tender, drain, lay it in a deep dish, and pour over it the hot dressing. Cover and set aside to cool, then stand in the ice-chest for an hour or two before serving.

Asparagus loaf

Cook three cupfuls of the asparagus tips until tender, then drain. Put into a saucepan two tablespoonfuls of butter and one tablespoonful of flour; cook together one minute. Add one cupful of milk, one-half teaspoonful of salt and one-fourth teaspoonful of paprika. Add the milk slowly, stirring all the time, and let it cook five minutes. Take from the fire and add four well-beaten eggs, one cupful of asparagus tips and a teaspoonful of chopped parsley. Line a well-buttered baking dish with the remainder of the asparagus tips; pour in the asparagus and sauce, and cook with the dish in water in the oven for fifteen minutes. Serve with egg sauce.

ARTICHOKES

The American artichoke, indigenous to this country, has received, nobody living can say why, the absurd name of "Jerusalem artichoke." It is a tuber, resembling in appearance a turnip when cooked, but far more agreeable in flavor.

The Italian artichoke *articiocco* was introduced into this country some years ago, and speedily became a fashionable edible. The part eaten is the succulent bud, cut before it expands into a flower.

Boiled Jerusalem artichokes

Wash the artichokes thoroughly, pare and slice or trim them into an oblong shape. Cook in slightly salted boiling water until tender, but not broken, and pour melted butter over them. Sprinkle with salt and pepper, and when turned into the dish, add a sprinkling of minced parsley and a few drops of lemon juice.

Baked Jerusalem artichokes

Wash and pare the artichokes, and cook tender. Then cut into neat slices. Put them into a baking-dish, sprinkle on a layer of grated Parmesan cheese and cover with a white or cream sauce. Sprinkle buttered crumbs over the top and bake until the crumbs are brown.

Boiled Italian artichokes

Cut off the stems, put the vegetables into boiling salted water, and boil for half-an-hour. Cut in half from top to bottom and serve half-an-one to each person. Pass with them a Hollandaise sauce. The stems are stripped off by the person eating the artichoke, the soft end dipped in the sauce and eaten. The fuzzy part should be scraped off and the bottom of the artichoke, which is really the most delicate portion, eaten with a fork.

Italian artichokes with sauce tartare

Remove the stems and outer leaves from the artichokes, and with a sharp knife remove the cores or centers. Lay these in cold, salted water for half-an-hour, drain and put into a saucepan with enough salted, boiling water to cover them. Cook until tender, drain thoroughly, put into a heated vegetable dish, and pour over them a sauce made of a half-cupful of melted butter, into which you have beaten a teaspoonful of lemon juice, a few drops of onion juice, a saltspoonful of French mustard, a pinch, each, of salt and paprika, and a teaspoonful of salad oil. Beat this sauce all together over the fire, remove from the range, and stir it, very slowly, into one beaten egg. Unless this is done gradually, the hot liquid will curdle the egg. Beat hard for a minute before pouring over the artichokes.

Fried Italian artichokes

Cut off the leaves and trim away the wool from the stalks. Cook tender, but not until broken, in salted water; drain and set on ice until perfectly cold. Make a good batter of half a cupful of flour sifted twice with a quarter teaspoonful of baking-powder and a little salt, wet up with half a cupful of milk into which has been beaten one egg.

Cut each artichoke, perpendicularly, into halves, sprinkle with salt and pepper, dip into the batter and fry in deep cottolene or other fat. Drain off every drop of fat and serve hot with a tart sauce.

BANANAS

Bananas sautés

Peel, cut lengthwise into thirds; roll in flour, slightly salted and peppered. Heat two tablespoonfuls of butter, or clarified dripping in a frying-pan; put in the bananas and fry to a golden brown, turning several times. Serve upon buttered toast.

Bananas fried whole

Peel and cut off the tip at each end; sprinkle with pepper and salt, roll in beaten egg, then in fine crumbs, again in egg, and again crumb them. Leave them upon ice for an hour or two, and fry in deep, boiling cottolene or other fat to a delicate brown. Serve very hot.

Baked bananas

Strip off one-third of the skin of each, and with a silver knife loosen the skin around the fruit. Arrange in a baking-pan with the stripped side uppermost. On each banana place a quarter teaspoonful of butter, sprinkle with one teaspoonful of sugar and a half teaspoonful of water for each banana, and bake about twenty minutes.

Scalloped bananas

Peel, slice and arrange in a buttered bake-dish, alternately with fine crumbs. Sprinkle each layer with salt, pepper and butter, also with a little cream. Let the uppermost layer be crumbs, well-buttered and wet with cream. Bake, covered, half-an-hour, then brown.

BEANS

Boston baked beans (No. 1)

Soak a quart of beans in cold water all night. In the morning soak them for two hours in warm water. Drain, put into a pot with enough water to cover them, and bring them slowly to a boil. When they are tender, turn then into a deep bake-dish; first pouring off the surplus water. Cut gashes in a half-pound piece of parboiled salt pork, and place this in the center of the dish. To a pint of the water in which the beans were boiled add a gill of molasses and a saltspoonful of French mustard. Mix well, and pour this over the beans and pork. Cover the dish and bake in a steady oven for six hours.

Boston baked beans (No. 2)

Wash a quart of beans, let them stand over-night in a gallon of cold water. In the morning, pour off the water and wash again. Then place in a pot, cover with plenty of water, and set over the fire.

Have the pork all fat if possible, unless lean is preferred. Score the rind deeply. Put the beans and pork over the fire and simmer until the beans begin to crack open, not any longer. Drain all the water from them and rinse again with cold water. Put about half the beans in the pot, and then the pork, rind-side up. Next, put in the remainder of the beans. Mix a teaspoonful, each, of mustard and sugar with pepper, and a great spoonful of molasses with a pint of boiling water and pour over the beans. Cover the pot, set in a slow oven and bake ten hours, adding boiling water whenever the beans look dry. Do not have the fire so hot that the water on the beans bubbles, and have no more water than will barely come to the top of the beans. Use an earthen pot.

New Jersey baked beans

Soak and boil the beans in the same way as before described—only change the water in which they are boiled an hour before they are done—and boil the pork with the beans; a slice of onion and a tiny piece of bay-leaf may be added to the first water. When they are ready for baking fill a shallow basin with them; place the pork in the center with the scored rind exposed, with one or two tablespoonfuls of molasses, some white pepper, and one tablespoonful of butter in small bits sprinkled all over the beans; bake, covered, about two hours. Enough of the water in which they were boiled should be poured in to make them soft, and about an hour before they are done one cupful of sweet cream, heated, with a pinch of soda, may be poured in upon the beans, loosening them with a fork that the cream may soak in.

Sunnybank baked beans

Soak over night and boil tender as already directed. Parboil half a pound of pork and chop fine. Have ready a large cupful of strained tomato sauce, well seasoned with onion juice, butter, salt and a good deal of sugar. Put a layer of minced pork in the bottom of your dish; then one of beans, next tomato sauce. Proceed in this way until the dish is full; add a very little hot water; cover closely and bake two hours, then brown.

It will be found very good, a vast improvement upon the conventional pork and baked beans. The top layer should be of tomato sauce.

Baked beans with tomato sauce

Soak white beans over night in cold water, and in the morning put over the fire in boiling water, slightly salted. Cook until tender. Drain and put into a deep dish. Cover with a tomato sauce, made by cooking together a tablespoonful, each, of butter and flour until they bubble, and then pouring upon them a cupful of strained tomato liquor. Season to taste, and rather highly, unless you have previously added salt and pepper to the beans. Stir the sauce in with these and bake, closely covered, for two hours.

Beans sautés

Soak beans over night and boil until tender. Drain very dry and sprinkle with salt. Put two tablespoonfuls of butter into a frying pan, and when this has melted fry in it a large onion sliced. When the onion has browned remove it with a perforated spoon, and stir into the butter a tablespoonful of minced parsley. Now add the beans and turn them over and over in the hissing butter until very hot. Sprinkle lightly with salt (if needed) and pepper. Turn into a colander, then into a hot dish.

Stewed beans

Soak over night. In the morning parboil for one hour, drain, put them over the fire in enough weak stock to cover them and stew two hours, slowly. For the last hour set in a pan of boiling water to prevent scorching. All the stock should be absorbed, yet the beans should not be dry. At the end of two hours stir in a sauce made of one tablespoonful of butter, one teaspoonful of mustard and the same of molasses, with twice as much onion juice and the juice of half a lemon, mixed in half a cupful of boiling water. Leave, covered, upon the fire for ten minutes (still in boiling water) and turn out.

Lima beans

Shell, lay in cold water for half an hour, and cook half an hour in boiling water, a little salted. Drain, dish, toss about over a lump of butter, and salt and pepper to your liking.

Lima beans with white sauce

Cook as directed in last recipe, but instead of dishing after draining, return to the saucepan with a good white sauce into which you have stirred a little chopped parsley. Simmer three minutes and serve.

Boiled string beans

You can not destroy this dish more effectually than by "stringing" the beans in the slovenly manner practised by at least one-half of American cooks, or those who represent the American kitchen. The neatest way of ridding beans of backbones is to pare each the whole length with a sharp knife. The flavor is more delicate when this is done.

Lay a handful of the pods upon a board with the ends even, and cut through all into inch-pieces. Wash and cook in boiling salted water until tender. Drain, season with butter, salt and pepper, and serve.

Full-grown beans demand much more time for cooking than young. Underdone beans have a rank taste and are unwholesome.

Steamed cream string beans

By some they are called "butter beans," by others "German wax beans." They are sweeter and richer than the ordinary green string bean. Put into cold water for half an hour after paring the fiber lightly from each side of the pods, taking care not to touch the beans inside. Then, with a *sharp* knife cut them into slanting slivers, three for each bean, and each a little over an inch long. Wash and put the dripping beans into a saucepan containing a great spoonful of warmed (not hot) butter, pepper and salt to taste. Add three tablespoonfuls of warm water. Cover closely, and bring slowly to a gentle simmer. Now and then shake the saucepan upward to make sure the beans are not sticking to the bottom, but do not open it, as everything depends upon the steam. Young beans may be tender in forty minutes. Large or stale will not be fit to eat under one hour. Do not put more than three tablespoonfuls of water for a quart of beans, and dish without draining.

String beans of any kind are nicer when cooked in this way than any other.

Savory string beans

String and cut the beans diagonally as just directed, and boil tender in salted water. Have ready a roux of butter and flour, and mix it with half a cupful of gravy of any kind. Stir until smooth, seasoning with pepper, salt and a little onion. Strain this sauce over the beans and cook for five minutes longer.

BEETS

Boiled beets

As the preliminary process to all dishes composed of beets is boiling it is well to learn exactly how this should be done. Too often the once ruddy vegetable is allowed to "bleed" out its juices until it has a pallid and uninviting appearance.

Wash the beets, rubbing them carefully with the palm of the hand to dislodge dirt, but not so hard as to abrade the tender skin. Drop into fresh cold water as you cleanse them. Put into a saucepan of salted boiling water and cook for an hour. Drain, scrape, slice and serve in a deep dish with melted butter poured over them. They are best when a tablespoonful of hot vinegar is added to the melted butter.

Creamed young beets

Cook with two inches of the stem on to prevent bleeding, and do not clip the tap root. Have ready a cupful of cream heated with a pinch of soda. Rub the skins off, top and tail the beets, and slice them thin into the cream, setting the saucepan containing it in boiling water. When all are in stir in a tablespoonful of butter rubbed into one of flour, pepper, salt and a teaspoonful, each, of sugar and onion juice. Simmer two minutes to cook the flour, and dish.

BRUSSELS SPROUTS

Boiled Brussels sprouts

Remove the outer leaves and lay the sprouts in cold salted water for three-quarters of an hour. Drain and boil in salted water for about fifteen minutes, or until tender. Try with a fork, and if they are tender, but not soft, all through, they are done. Drain and lay in a hot dish and pour over them a half cupful of melted butter in which has been stirred a half saltspoonful, each, of salt and pepper. Serve very hot.

Brussels sprouts au gratin

Boil the sprouts tender in salted water, drain and cut each sprout in four pieces. Cook together a tablespoonful, each, of butter and flour, and when they are blended pour upon them a scant pint of milk. When you have a smooth sauce stir the quartered sprouts into this. Season to taste, turn all into a greased pudding-dish, strew thickly with crumbs and bits of butter, and bake to a light brown. Serve in the dish in which they were baked.

CABBAGE

Those who know cabbage as it is served with the old-fashioned "boiled dinner" have no conception of the many delightful changes of which this so-called plebeian vegetable is susceptible. In summer, when it is young and tender, it is particularly good, and may be so cooked that it is as palatable and delicate to the taste as its refined cousin, the cauliflower. Have the water boiling when the vegetable is thrust into it, head down, and keep it at a hard boil until done. Some housekeepers claim that a teaspoonful of vinegar added to the water will dissipate the obnoxious odor.

Savory boiled cabbage

Cut a firm cabbage into four parts and reject the outer leaves. Wash carefully in two waters, taking care to dislodge any insects that may be concealed between the leaves. Have a large pot of boiling water on the range; dissolve in a tablespoonful of salt and a quarter of a teaspoonful of baking soda. Plunge the cabbage into this, and cook, uncovered, for fifteen minutes, drain, and fill the pot with more boiling water, adding salt as you do so. Cook the cabbage until tender, always uncovered, turn into a colander, press out all the water and set aside to get very cold. Chop fine and season with salt, white pepper, and a dash of tomato catsup. Heat in a saucepan a large cupful of well-seasoned soup stock, turn the cabbage into this and toss and turn until very hot. Now add a large spoonful of melted butter, and a teaspoonful of lemon juice, and serve.

Baked cabbage

Boil cabbage tender in two waters, drain and set aside until cold, then chop fine. Mix together two beaten eggs, two tablespoonfuls of melted butter, two tablespoonfuls of cream, a saltspoonful of salt and a dash of paprika. Stir this into the chopped cabbage and put it into a buttered pudding-dish. Sprinkle breadcrumbs over the top and bake until brown.

Fricasseed cabbage

Boil and chop, as in the last recipe, and keep hot while you cook together in a saucepan a tablespoonful of butter and one (heaping) of flour; when they bubble pour upon them a cupful of hot milk. Stir to a smooth sauce; turn into this the chopped cabbage, cook for a minute, season and serve.

Stuffed cabbage

Choose a fresh, firm cabbage. Lay in cold water for half an hour, and boil in salted water for ten minutes. Remove, drain, and allow it to get very cold. Meanwhile make a forcemeat of a cupful of boiled rice and the same quantity of chopped cold chicken with half a cupful of minced ham. Work to a paste and season. Stand the cabbage on the stem-end and carefully open the leaves, beginning at the center. Fill the spaces between the layers of leaves with the forcemeat; close the cabbage upon itself, tie it up firmly in a piece of coarse netting, put it gently into a pot of boiling salted water, and cook almost two hours. Take from the water, remove the netting very carefully, put the cabbage on a platter and pour a rich white sauce over it. If properly prepared, this is a delicious dish.

Baked cabbage with tomato sauce

Boil a cabbage in two waters, drain, cut it fine, and season with salt and pepper. Grease a pudding-dish and put a layer of the cabbage in the bottom of it; cover this layer with tomato sauce and sprinkle with a few fine crumbs. Proceed in this way until the dish is full, having the last layer of crumbs. Bake for half an hour.

Shredded cabbage and cheese

Cut a cabbage into shreds and boil in salted water until tender. Drain and stand in a heated colander at the side of the range. Cook together two teaspoonfuls of butter and two of flour, and pour upon them a pint of hot milk. Season with salt and pepper, and stir in three heaping tablespoonfuls of grated cheese. Cook, stirring constantly, for just a minute. Turn the cabbage into a deep vegetable dish and pour the cheese sauce over it.

Cold slaw

Wash a cabbage and lay it in cold water for half an hour. With a sharp knife cut it into strips, or shreds. As you cut these drop them into iced water. When ready to serve, drain in a colander, shaking hard to dislodge the moisture, and pour over all a dressing made by rubbing the yolks of two hard-boiled eggs to a paste with one beaten egg, a half cupful of salad oil, the juice of a lemon, mustard, salt and pepper to taste.

Cabbage cream salad

Prepare as in the preceding recipe, only cutting the shreds into inch-lengths before dropping them in iced water. Beat a pint of cream very stiff. Drain the cabbage, sprinkle lightly with salt, and stir it into the whipped cream, turning and tossing until it is thoroughly coated with the white foam. Serve at once with crackers and cheese. The cabbage should be tender and crisp for this dish.

An Italian dish of cabbage

Boil a cabbage in two waters; drain; when cold, chop coarsely, and season with salt and pepper. Butter a pudding-dish, put a layer of the cabbage in this; sprinkle with buttered crumbs and a teaspoonful of grated Parmesan cheese. Put in more cabbage, more crumbs and cheese, and, when the dish is nearly full, pour a cup of seasoned beef stock over all. Bake for half an hour.

Scalloped cabbage

Boil a head of cabbage in two waters; drain; let it cool, and chop fine. Cover the bottom of a baking-dish with bread-crumbs; scatter over these tiny morsels of butter, seasoned with pepper, salt and a few drops of onion juice; spread with a layer, an inch thick, of the minced cabbage. Season this layer with salt, butter-bits, and a sharp dash of lemon juice. Repeat the crumbs, then a second stratum of cabbage, a cupful of boiling milk, and cover all thickly with bread-dust, well seasoned. Sift grated cheese upon the top, and bake, covered, until bubbling hot. Uncover and brown. You can use weak stock in place of milk if you have it. Boil a pinch of soda in the milk. An excellent family dish.

CARROTS

Stewed carrots

Wash, scrape off the skin, cut into dice and leave in cold water for half an hour. Put, then, into the inner compartment of a double boiler with no water upon them except that which clings to them after washing. Cover closely, and cook tender. An hour should be long enough for this. Turn into a deep dish, pepper and salt, and cover with a good white sauce.

Mashed carrots

Scrape and slice carrots, and boil tender in two waters. Drain, rub through a colander, and mash with a potato-beetle. Beat light with a tablespoonful of melted butter, add salt and pepper, and serve very hot.

Carrots sautés

Boil young carrots, not longer than your forefinger, for eight minutes in salted water. Rub and scrape off the skins; cover with boiling water and cook tender. Drain, lay for a minute in cold water until you can handle them, and cut each carrot in two, each half into strips. Heat a tablespoonful of butter in a frying-pan with a half teaspoonful of white sugar, a little salt and pepper, and when it boils lay in the strips of carrot. Cook three minutes after the bubble recommences; sprinkle with chopped parsley, toss about for one minute, drain and serve hot.

Carrot croquettes

Wash and scrape and cook until very tender. Mash smooth and beat to a paste with the yolk of a raw egg, a good spoonful of softened butter, pepper and salt to taste. Let this paste get cold and stiff before making into croquettes or balls. Roll in beaten egg, then in fine crumbs; set on ice for an hour and fry in deep, boiling cottolene or other fat. Drain and serve hot.

CAULIFLOWER

Cauliflower boiled whole

Choose a fine, white head for this purpose. Put it, flower downward, into ice-cold salted water for half an hour. Tie, then, in coarse cheese-cloth or netting, and plunge, head fore most, into a pot of boiling salted water. Cook half an hour, drain, take off the cloth and dish. Pour a rich white sauce over it.

Cauliflower au gratin

Cut a large cauliflower into eight pieces and boil tender in salted water. Drain, lay in a deep pudding-dish, stems down, and pour over it a plain white sauce into which two hard-boiled eggs have been chopped. Sprinkle with bread-crumbs and bake to a light brown.

Cauliflower with tomato sauce

Boil a whole cauliflower for ten minutes in fresh water; drain and boil until tender in salted water. Put into a vegetable dish, flower side up, rub thoroughly with butter, then sprinkle with salt and pepper. Last of all, pour over the cauliflower a pint of tomato sauce.

CELERY

Stewed celery (No. 1)

Wash the celery, cut into half-inch bits, and stew tender in slightly-salted boiling water. Drain this off and add a cupful of milk. Cook for three minutes, stir in a teaspoonful of butter rubbed into a teaspoonful of flour, boil up once, season to taste, and serve.

Stewed celery (No. 2)

A bunch of indifferent celery may be utilized for this dish. I have rescued stalks frosted accidentally through the cook's carelessness, laid them in ice-cold water for two hours, prepared them as I shall direct, and presented as palatable food that whose end would otherwise have been the garbage pail.

After stewing tender and draining, transfer to another saucepan in which you have heated a cupful of milk (with a pinch of soda in it), thicken it with a tablespoonful of butter rubbed in a teaspoonful of flour, and stir to a boil. Mix the celery well with this, season with pepper and salt, heat all together for one minute, and dish.

Brown stew of celery

Wash and cut into small bits a bunch of celery. Put it into a saucepan and pour over it a pint of cleared beef stock. Stew until tender. Drain the celery and set aside while you return to the saucepan the stock in which it was cooked. Thicken this with a paste made by rubbing a heaping teaspoonful of browned flour into one teaspoonful of butter. When you have a smooth brown sauce, stir in the celery, and when this is very hot, season and serve.

Savory celery

Scrape, cut into inch-lengths, lay in cold water for an hour; cook tender in salted hot water. Drain, and return the celery to the saucepan. Have ready heated a cupful of weak stock, or gravy, strained through a cloth, seasoned with paprika, salt and onion juice, then thickened with a tablespoonful of browned flour rolled in the same quantity of butter. Pour this over the celery, heat all together for one minute, and dish.

The outer green stalks of celery may be used thus, and more satisfactorily than a tyro might think possible.

Fried celery

Scrape and boil as directed in foregoing recipes; drain, and spread upon a cloth in a very cold place. They must be dry and firm before you dip each piece in beaten egg, then in seasoned bread or cracker-dust. Set again in the cold for an hour, and fry in deep cottolene or other fat to a golden brown. Drain in a hot colander and serve.

Stewed celery roots

Wash and scrape the roots of celery and stew in salted water until very tender. Drain and cut into small dice. Have ready in a saucepan a pint of hot milk, thicken this with a teaspoonful of flour rubbed into one of butter, turn a cupful (heaping) of the celery dice into this sauce, stir until very hot, season to taste and serve.

Besides being a palatable dish when thus cooked, celery root is an admirable nervine, and therefore indicated as beneficial diet for brainworkers and nervous invalids.

GREEN CORN

Boiled corn

Strip husk and silk from the ear and put over the fire in plenty of boiling water, slightly salted. Boil hard for twenty minutes if the corn be young and fresh.

Send to table wrapped in a napkin.

Stewed corn

Cut from the cob with a sharp knife; put over the fire in just enough boiling salted water to cover it. Stew gently ten minutes; turn off the water and add a cupful of hot milk (with a pinch of soda in it). Cook ten minutes more, stir in a tablespoonful of butter rubbed up with a teaspoonful of flour; boil one minute and turn into a hot, deep dish.

Green corn pudding (No. 1)

Grate the grains from twelve ears of corn; beat into the corn the whipped yolks of four eggs until thoroughly incorporated; stir in now two tablespoonfuls of melted butter and one tablespoonful of powdered sugar; salt to taste, and add the whites of the eggs whipped to a froth. Lastly stir in a tiny pinch of soda; turn into a buttered pudding-dish and bake, covered, half an hour. Uncover, brown quickly, and send to table at once.

If this delicious "soufflé" be made of canned corn, chop it very fine.

Green corn pudding (No. 2)

Mix together two cupfuls of grated corn, two beaten eggs, a half pint of milk, a pinch of soda, a tablespoonful of melted butter and a tablespoonful of sugar. Grease a shallow baking-dish, turn the mixture into this, sprinkle with buttered crumbs, cover and bake for half an hour, then uncover and brown.

Green corn pudding (No. 3)

Grate the kernels from twelve ears of corn and stir into them the beaten yolks of six eggs and a tablespoonful, each, of melted butter and granulated sugar. Now beat in a quart of milk, a half teaspoonful of salt and, last of all, the stiffened whites of the six eggs. Turn into a greased pudding-dish and bake, covered, for half an hour, then uncover and brown.

This, when properly made and baked in a quick oven, is a veritable soufflé and incomparable.

Corn fritters

Cut from the ears a pint of sweet corn. Beat together a cupful of milk, two tablespoonfuls of melted butter, one egg, whipped light, salt to taste and enough flour to make a thin batter. Into this stir the grated corn. Beat hard and cook as you would griddle-cakes upon a soapstone griddle. They are a palatable accompaniment to roast chicken.

Green corn balls

Grate enough green corn from the cob to make two cupfuls; into this stir a beaten egg, a teaspoonful, each, of sugar and melted butter, with salt to taste. Add enough flour to enable you to form the mixture into balls, roll these in flour and fry in deep fat.

Succotash

Cut the corn from eight ears and put it into a saucepan with a pint of young Lima beans and enough salted boiling water to cover them both. Boil until the vegetables are tender; drain and turn into a double boiler with a cupful of boiling milk. Cook for ten minutes, then stir in a tablespoonful of butter, and simmer for five minutes longer. Season to taste and serve. Large "Limas" should be cooked ten minutes before the corn is added.

Corn and tomatoes

Grate the grains from six ears of corn; pare and cut into small pieces four ripe tomatoes. Put over the fire in a saucepan; stew half an hour; season with a great spoonful of butter, a teaspoonful of sugar and one of onion juice; salt and pepper to taste. Cook five minutes more and dish.

Scallop of corn and tomatoes

Pare and cut small a dozen ripe tomatoes and turn them, or the contents of a can of tomatoes, into a chopping bowl and chop the large pieces of the vegetable into small bits; then set in a saucepan over the fire and bring to the boil. Drain the liquor from a can of corn, or grate the grains from a dozen ears, and put the corn into a bowl of fresh water. After ten minutes drain the water off, and transfer the corn to a saucepan with enough boiling water to cover it. Let it simmer for five minutes, pour off the water and add the boiling tomatoes to the corn. Let both cook together for five minutes, during which time stir into them a heaping teaspoonful of butter, two teaspoonfuls of granulated sugar, and salt and pepper to taste. Pour the mixture into a greased bake-dish, sprinkle bread-crumbs and bits of butter over the top and bake for half an hour.

Green corn croquettes

Grate the corn from a dozen ears, or drain the liquor from a can of corn, and chop the kernels fine. Cook together a tablespoonful of butter and two of flour, and, when these are blended, add slowly a pint of milk into which has been stirred a pinch of soda. Cook this mixture, stirring all the time, until you have a thick white sauce; add to it the chopped corn and half a tea spoonful of powdered sugar, with pepper and salt to taste. Remove from the fire and set aside to cool. When cold, form with lightly-floured hands into croquettes, and dip each croquette in beaten egg and cracker-dust. Set all aside in a platter in the ice-chest for several hours, then fry in deep, boiling fat.

Corn omelet

Grate the corn from four ears of boiled corn. Beat four eggs well, add three tablespoonfuls of cream and cook in a hot pan. When ready to fold, sprinkle with salt and pepper, add the corn and turn out on a hot dish. Heat the corn slightly over hot water before putting into the omelet.

Creole chowder

Heat a generous lump of butter and in it brown four sliced onions. Add four peeled tomatoes, four chopped green bell-peppers, and the corn cut from four cobs. Add as much water as may be needed in cooking, season with salt and sugar and a little black pepper. A full hour's cooking will be necessary, and the chowder must be served piping hot.

CUCUMBERS

Many persons look upon the cucumber with fear as a source of indigestion and gastric discomfort. One able dietitian has left on record his opinion that a square inch of verdant cucumber is about as fit to be put into the human stomach as would be a like quantity of Paris green.

Our cucumber, like many another abused article, is maligned because its enemies have never made the attempt to do it justice. If a few simple rules are followed it will prove less indigestible and more palatable than foes and friends imagine. When cooked, it loses many of its disturbing qualities. But, as some people enjoy the crisp freshness of its raw state, it is well to learn just how to prepare it properly.

Raw cucumbers

See to it that the cucumber is fresh and lay it on the ice until wanted. Do not be content with leaving it on the shelf of the refrigerator. It must be in actual contact with the ice. Just before sending to the table, peel quickly and slice thin, scattering crushed ice among the slices. At the table make a French dressing of one part vinegar, three parts oil, salt and pepper to taste, and pour over the cucumbers as you dish them. To allow the vegetable to lie for even fifteen minutes in the dressing is to toughen the fiber and make it as indigestible as gutta percha.

Stewed cucumbers

Peel eight medium-sized cucumbers and cut them into slices an inch thick. Lay in iced water for half an hour. Have a pint of unsalted, hot beef stock in a saucepan, drain the cucumbers and lay them in this. Stew until tender, then remove with a skimmer and lay in a vegetable-dish. Cook together a tablespoonful, each, of butter and browned flour, and pour upon them the stock in which the cucumbers were cooked. Stir until you have a smooth brown sauce; add a saltspoonful of salt, the same amount of pepper, a teaspoonful of kitchen bouquet and a half teaspoonful of onion juice. Stir all together and pour over the stewed cucumbers.

Stuffed cucumbers

Cut good-sized young cucumbers into halves, lengthwise, and remove the seeds. Fill the hollows thus left with a forcemeat made of equal parts of chopped roast beef and minced boiled ham, with half as much fine bread-crumbs. Moisten this stuffing with melted butter and season to taste. Place the halves of each cucumber carefully together and tie with soft twine. Place in a roasting-pan, pour about them a cupful of skimmed beef stock, and cook until tender. Remove the strings, transfer the cucumbers to a hot platter, thicken the gravy left in the pan and pour it about them. This is a Syrian recipe.

Baked cucumbers

Peel medium-sized cucumbers, arrange them in a bake-dish and pour about them a couple of tablespoonfuls of water in which has been melted a tablespoonful of butter. Dust with salt and pepper, and bake, covered, for half an hour. If you wish, you can scallop them by cutting them in slices, sprinkling with crumbs and basting with bits of butter. Bake, covered, until tender; uncover and brown.

Fried cucumbers

Peel and leave in ice water for half an hour. Slice lengthwise, making three slices of each cucumber of fair size, lay in fresh iced water for ten minutes more. Wipe dry, sprinkle with pepper and salt, dredge with flour and fry to a light brown in deep, boiling cottolene or other fat. Drain, and serve dry and hot.

CHESTNUTS

The large Spanish chestnuts sold by grocers in the city, and in the markets, make excellent puddings with or without sugar, and, as vegetables, go well with poultry and beef.

Chestnut pudding

Boil and skin enough chestnuts to make a cupful when rubbed through a colander or vegetable press. Beat four eggs light, stir the chestnut into the yolks; add a tablespoonful of melted butter and two tablespoonfuls of fine cracker dust, two cupfuls of milk, a tablespoonful of sugar, salt and pepper to taste; lastly, the frothed whites. Bake, covered, in a buttered pudding-dish for half an hour; uncover, brown and serve before it falls. Eat with meat.

Chestnut croquettes

Shell and boil five cupfuls of large chestnuts; skin, and rub through a colander. Work into them a tablespoonful of butter, a little salt, a few drops of lemon juice and a dash of paprika. Turn into a double boiler, and make very hot, then set aside to cool. When cold form into small croquettes, roll in egg, then in cracker-crumbs and set in the ice for an hour before frying in deep, boiling cottolene or other fat. Peanut croquettes may be made in the same way.

DANDELIONS

Make a wholesome and, to some tastes, palatable "greens" in the spring of the year. They must be gathered while very young and tender, or they are bitter. The best time to cut them is just before they flower. Throw at once into cold water, as they wilt soon after they are picked.

Stewed dandelions (No. 1)

Cut the stems from a half peck of dandelion leaves, and break each leaf into small bits, dropping these into cold water as you do so. Wash thoroughly, drain, and lay in cold water for fifteen minutes. Drain again, and put over the fire in a porcelain-lined saucepan, with enough salted water to cover them. Simmer for fifteen minutes while you make the following sauce:

Cook together a tablespoonful, each, of butter and flour, and pour upon them a pint of milk, in which a pinch of soda has been dissolved. Stir to a smooth white sauce. Drain the water from the dandelion leaves, and stir these into the sauce. Season to taste, and beat in, very slowly, a whipped egg. Remove at once from the fire and turn into a deep vegetable dish.

Stewed dandelions (No. 2)

Pick the leaves from the stems, and drop into iced water. Take them up by the handful, dripping wet, and put, with no other water, into the inner vessel of a farina boiler. Fill the outer kettle with boiling water; cover the inner closely, and cook fast for half an hour. Rub the leaves through a vegetable press or a col ander into a saucepan; beat in a tablespoonful of butter, a teaspoonful of sugar, salt and pepper to taste, a teaspoonful of lemon juice, and, at the last, three tablespoonfuls of hot cream to which has been added a pinch of soda. Stir until smoking hot over the fire, turn out into a heated dish, garnish with sippets of fried bread, and serve.

Dandelion greens cooked thus are almost as good as spinach *à la crême*.

EGGPLANT—A MUCH ABUSED VEGETABLE

Tens of thousands of average American housewives know but one way of cooking it, and not one in a hundred performs that one properly.

Fried eggplant is one of the many dishes which remind the eater of the small girl of nursery-rhyme fame, who—

"When she was good was very, very good
But when she was bad she was horrid."

When only half fried, or soaked with grease, this vegetable is an abomination to the educated palate and the self-respecting stomach. When tender and thoroughly cooked, it is one of the most delicious of the summer and fall garden products.

Fried eggplant

Peel an eggplant and cut into slices half an inch thick. Lay in cold salt water for an hour; wipe each slice dry and dip, first in beaten egg, and then in cracker dust. Set in a cold place for an hour and fry in deep boiling cottolene or other fat. Drain in a heated colander before dishing.

Stuffed eggplant on the half-shell

Wash and wipe a large eggplant and parboil it in boiling salted water for ten minutes. Let it get perfectly cold, cut in half lengthwise, and scrape out the center, leaving the walls of the vegetable three-quarters of an inch thick. Chop the pulp fine and add to it a small cupful of minced chicken, half a cupful of minced ham, a quarter of a cupful of bread-crumbs, a tablespoonful of melted butter, salt and pepper to taste. Mix well, add enough soup stock to make a stiff paste, and fill the hollow sides with this. When full and rounded, sprinkle the forcemeat with bread-crumbs, and lay the halves, side by side, in a bakepan, pouring three cupfuls of soup stock around them. Bake nearly an hour, basting every ten minutes. Remove the eggplant to a hot platter, thicken the gravy left in the pan with browned flour, boil up once on top of the range, stirring constantly, and pour this browned sauce about the base of the halved eggplant.

Scalloped eggplant

Pare off the skin, cut into dice and lay in cold salt water for an hour. Then parboil for twenty minutes. Drain well and pack in a buttered bake-dish, alternately, with fine crumbs. Dot each layer with butter, sprinkle with salt and pepper, and strew with finely-minced sweet green peppers. Fill the dish in this order, cover with a layer of crumbs wet with cream; dot with butter, cover and bake half an hour, then brown.

Eggplant stuffed with tomatoes

Halve the eggplant and remove the insides as in the last recipe but one. Make a forcemeat of the eggplant pulp, a cupful of chopped ripe tomatoes, one chopped green pepper, and a cupful of bread-crumbs. Season with a tablespoonful of melted butter and salt and pepper. Fill the hollow sides with this mixture, bind the two halves together with wide tape, and bake, basting frequently with melted butter and hot water. When tender, transfer to a hot platter, cut and remove the tape, and pour hot tomato sauce about the eggplant.

Stewed eggplant, with sauce piquante

Prepare as for eggplant on the half-shell by halving and scooping out the pulp, leaving substantial walls. Chop the pulp and cover with hot water. Season with a tablespoonful of onion juice, salt and pepper, and simmer for fifteen minutes. Take from the fire, drain, turn into a bowl and work in two tablespoonfuls of soft bread-crumbs, one tablespoonful of finely-chopped capers, two tablespoonfuls of cold boiled tongue, minced, and, when well-mixed, add salt to taste.

Pack this forcemeat closely into each half, and fit the two parts together, binding securely together with tapes or soft twine.

Put into your covered roaster; pour enough weak stock around it to come one-third of the way up the side, bake, covered, half an hour, then turn and cook the other side. Undo the strings, lay the eggplant carefully in the middle of a hot dish, and pour a good sauce piquante over and around it.

HOMINY

The small-grained hominy, called at the South "samp," after the manner of the aborigines who bequeathed it to us, must be used in the recipes which follow.

Plain hominy pudding

Soak a cupful of hominy for three hours in tepid water. Drain, and put over the fire in plenty of boiling water, slightly salted. Boil fast for thirty minutes or until tender; turn off the water and pour in a pint of hot milk, with a little salt. Cook for fifteen minutes, stir in a generous lump of butter and turn into a deep dish.

Eat with sugar and cream.

Baked hominy

Stir into a pint of milk a cupful of cold boiled hominy, and when this is smooth, add a tablespoonful of melted butter, a tablespoon ful of sugar, a saltspoonful of salt and four well-beaten eggs. Beat very light, pour into a buttered pudding-dish and bake for about half an hour or until "set" and brown. This is a good accompaniment to roast beef.

Hominy croquettes

Into two cupfuls of boiled hominy work a tablespoonful of melted butter; when the cereal is free from all lumps, add to it two beaten eggs, and when these are thoroughly incorporated, season the mixture with salt and pepper. Flour your hands, make the paste into small croquettes, and set aside until stiff and very cold. Now dip each croquette into beaten egg, roll in cracker-crumbs, and when all are thoroughly coated set in the ice-box for two hours. Fry to a golden brown in deep, boiling cottolene or other fat.

Hominy fritters

Rub two cupfuls of cold boiled hominy to a smooth paste with one tablespoonful of melted butter. Next, thin with warmed milk, and add three well-beaten eggs. Finally, stir in a cupful of flour which has been sifted twice with a teaspoonful of salt and half as much baking-powder.

Drop by the spoonful into boiling, deep cottolene or other fat; or, better still, cook upon a soapstone griddle.

KALE

This vegetable, otherwise known as "sea-kale," should be better known in our country. In England it takes high rank and holds it creditably.

Pick it over carefully, clip off the stems and lay it in cold water for an hour. Drain, and put it into a saucepan full of salted boiling water. Cook until tender, drain and chop fine. Return to the saucepan with three tablespoonfuls of melted butter, salt and pepper to taste. Serve very hot on squares of buttered toast.

MACARONI

Few articles of diet are more toothsome and more wholesome than macaroni in its various forms when properly prepared. Like rice, it is so often miserably cooked that its excellent qualities are not generally recognized. Macaroni may be bought in several shapes, the large, or pipe-macaroni being perhaps the most common. Besides this there are the smaller and more delicate vermicelli, spaghetti and the flat ribbon, or egg-macaroni. Recipes for the cooking of one may be used in the preparation of any of the divers phases of this food.

Baked macaroni (No. 1)

Break into inch-lengths half a pound of macaroni. Boil it until tender in weak broth. Drain off the liquor; put the macaroni into a pudding-dish that will stand the fire; pour over it a half cupful of the stock in which it was boiled, and put a tablespoonful of butter, broken into small pieces, here and there through it. Sift over it fine bread-crumbs and grated cheese; dot with bits of butter and brown in the oven.

Baked macaroni (No. 2)

Break half a pound of macaroni into short lengths; cook until tender in boiling, salted water. It must be clear and soft, but not broken. Drain and put a layer in the bottom of a buttered pudding-dish. Dot with butter, sprinkle lightly with cayenne and salt to taste; cover with grated cheese, and on this dispose another layer of macaroni. Fill the dish in this order, having cheese for the top layer. Pour in a cupful of milk; cover, and bake half an hour. Uncover and brown.

Creamed macaroni

Put a cupful of macaroni into two quarts of boiling salted water and cook for twenty-five minutes, or until tender, but not broken. Drain off all the water and keep the macaroni hot in a covered dish while you make the cream sauce to pour over it. Cook together in a saucepan until they bubble, two teaspoonfuls of flour and the same quantity of butter; pour over them a pint of hot milk, and, as this thickens, stir into it two heaping tablespoonfuls of grated Parmesan cheese. Pour this sauce upon the macaroni just before serving, lifting the latter lightly with a fork that the creamy sauce may reach every part.

Macaroni with cheese sauce

Boil tender in salted water and drain. Cook together in a saucepan a great spoonful of butter and a cupful of grated Swiss cheese. As soon as the cheese is melted, turn the macaroni into the saucepan and stir and toss with a silver fork until thoroughly blended with the sauce. Serve at once.

Macaroni and chicken

Boil half a package of spaghetti tender, drain, drop into cold water, and drain again. Lay on a biscuit-board and cut into pieces about half an inch long. Thicken a pint of chicken stock with a tablespoonful of flour rubbed into one of butter. Stir into this a cupful of cold boiled or roast chicken, chopped fine, and the cold macaroni. Last of all, beat in slowly a whipped egg, remove from the fire, season to taste, turn into a greased pudding-dish, sprinkle crumbs over the top and bake for half an hour.

Send around grated cheese with it. You may use veal if you have no chicken.

Macaroni and tomatoes (very nice)

Break half a pound of pipe macaroni into inch-lengths, and boil in salted water until tender. Drain, and put a layer of the macaroni in the bottom of a greased pudding-dish, sprinkle with pepper, salt, onion juice and grated cheese, and cover all with a layer of stewed and strained tomatoes that have been previously seasoned to taste. On these goes another layer of macaroni, and so on until the dish is full. The topmost layer must be of tomatoes sprinkled with crumbs and good-sized bits of butter. Set in a hot oven, covered, for twenty minutes, and then bake, uncovered, until the crumbs are well-browned.

Spaghetti with Swiss cheese

Break a half pound of spaghetti into bits not more than an inch and a half in length, and boil in slightly salted water for twenty minutes. Turn into a hot colander and set at the side of the range to drain. Grate enough Swiss cheese to make a generous half cupful and turn into a saucepan with three tablespoonfuls of melted butter. Stir well; add the hot spaghetti, toss and stir for a minute, or just long enough to melt the cheese; add a dash of paprika and serve in a hot dish.

Macaroni rissoles

Have ready a cupful of cold, boiled macaroni cut up small. Make a white sauce by cooking together a tablespoonful of butter and two of flour and stirring into them a cupful of hot milk. Stir until thick, add a large tablespoonful of grated cheese, and, gradually, the whipped yolks of four eggs, beating all the time. Work the macaroni into the sauce and set aside until the mixture is very cold. With floured hands form into small balls— not quite as large in circumference as a silver dollar—roll in beaten egg, then in fine cracker-crumbs, and set in the ice-box for two hours. Fry in deep, boiling cottolene or other fat. Serve with tomato sauce.

Macaroni piquante

Break spaghetti into very small bits less than an inch in length. Boil these for twenty minutes, or until tender, in salted water. Drain and keep hot while you make the following sauce:

Cook together in a saucepan a heaping teaspoonful, each, of butter and browned flour, and when these are blended to a brown roux, pour upon them a pint of beef stock, and stir until smooth. Now add four tablespoonfuls of tomato catsup, six drops of Tabasco sauce, a teaspoonful of kitchen bouquet, a pinch of salt and a dash of paprika. Turn the boiled spaghetti into this sauce, stir all together, and pour the mixture into a greased pudding-dish. Sprinkle buttered crumbs and grated cheese over the top and bake until brown.

Macaroni á la Napolitaine

Have a long fish kettle half full of boiling, salted water, and lay a half pound of unbroken pipe-macaroni in this. Boil for twenty minutes or until tender. Carefully drain the water from the kettle and slip the macaroni gently upon a heated platter, where it may lie at full length. Set the platter in the oven to keep warm while you make a sauce by cooking together in a saucepan two tablespoonfuls of butter and one of flour, and pouring upon them a pint of strained tomato liquor. Stir to a smooth sauce, then season with onion juice, celery salt, pepper, and four tablespoonfuls of Parmesan cheese. Pour this sauce over the macaroni on the platter. When you serve, cut the mass with a sharp knife into manageable lengths.

MUSHROOMS

It is a pity there should be such a popular dread of the poisonous "toadstool" that his nutritious and innocuous brother—the edible mushroom—is shunned by thousands of rational creatures. The most wary need not fear this joy of the epicure when it is bought at market or at a responsible grocer's shop. Trustworthy dealers run no risks in purchasing the wares from those whose business it is to cultivate and sell them. Mushrooms bought under these circumstances are no more to be feared than artichokes or Brussels sprouts. They form delicious entrées and tempt the most jaded appetite.

Broiled mushrooms

Peel carefully with a small knife and cut off the stems. Lay the mushrooms in a deep dish and pour melted butter over them. Remove them gently to a greased gridiron and broil over clear coals until delicately browned on both sides. Lay diamond-shaped slices of thin buttered toast in a dish, and the mushrooms upon these, sprinkle with pepper and salt and pour a little melted butter over all.

Fried mushrooms

Melt a great spoonful of butter in an agate frying-pan. Peel the mushrooms and cut off their stems, scraping the latter. Lay the mushrooms with their scraped stalks in the frying-pan and cook, turning often, until done. Serve very hot.

Stewed mushrooms

Peel the mushrooms and simmer gently in salted water until tender. Ten minutes should suffice. Drain and keep hot while you make a white sauce of a half pint of milk thickened with a tablespoonful of flour rubbed into one of butter. Turn the mushrooms into this and stir over the fire until very hot. Season with salt, pepper, a dash of mace, and serve.

Baked mushrooms

Peel very large mushrooms and cut off their stems. Grease a shallow pudding-dish and put a layer of mushrooms, under sides upward, into this. Into each mushroom pour a few drops of melted butter. Do not put more than two layers in the dish. Bake, closely covered, in a quick oven until tender. This should be in about twenty minutes. When done, remove the cover, pour melted butter over the mushrooms, and serve very hot in the dish in which they were cooked.

Fricasseed mushrooms

Peel and remove the stems from large mushrooms. Make a forcemeat by chopping the white meat of a cold roast chicken fine with a few small mushrooms and moistening it with chicken stock. Grease a pudding-dish and lay the large mushrooms, tops down, in this. Fill the mushrooms and the space between them with the forcemeat. Sprinkle bits of butter over all. Pour in enough of the chicken stock to make the contents of the dish very moist, lay a few wafer-like slices of bacon on top of the scallop, and bake, covered, in a hot oven for a quarter of an hour. Uncover, and cook for five minutes longer. Serve in the dish in which they were cooked.

ONIONS

A once-despised vegetable which now takes rank as a highly-respectable edible upon good men's—and women's—tables. Delicate spinsters no longer faint at fumes of boiled onions, and finical housewives have forgotten the rusty joke about cooking onions in the middle of a ten-acre lot. There are ways of extracting the coarser flavor that once condemned them with dyspeptics. Cooks have learned that there is as much difference between a well-done and a parboiled onion as between half-cooked and mealy potatoes. Housewives and physicians now appreciate the nutritive values of the esculent bulb, and prize it for these as well as for the seasoning which nothing else supplies. Onion juice is indispensable to the flavor of ragouts and soups, and is obtained by grating, not chopping. The superiority of this mode of getting the essence of the vegetable can not be rightly estimated by one who has not tried it. Onion seasoning should be tasted, never seen.

Stewed young onions

Cut off the stalks, remove the skins and lay the onions in cold water for half an hour. Put them over the fire in hot, salted water and cook for twenty minutes. Drain off the water and return the onions to the fire with a cupful of hot milk, in which has been dissolved a bit of soda the size of a pea. Add a tablespoonful of flour and stew slowly until the sauce is like thick cream.

Boiled onions

Peel and lay for an hour in cold water. Boil in two waters until tender. Drain, sprinkle with pepper and salt; put into a deep vegetable-dish and pour over them a great spoonful of melted butter.

Baked onions (No. 1)

Peel the onions and boil for ten minutes. Drain, arrange in a greased pudding-dish, sprinkle with salt and pepper, and pour over all a white sauce, to which a beaten egg has been added. Sprinkle with fine crumbs, set in the oven and bake, covered, for twenty minutes, then uncover and brown.

Baked onions (No. 2)

Cook tender in boiling water changed once after fifteen minutes; drain and arrange, side by side, in a baking-pan. Melt a tablespoonful of butter in a cupful of hot soup stock, season with salt and pepper and pour over the onions. Cook in a hot oven until the onions are brown, when they may be lifted with a perforated spoon and put into the dish in which they are to be served. Put the pan of gravy on top of the range, thicken the contents with browned flour and pour over the onions. Serve very hot.

Savory onions

Select young onions for this dish. Lay the onions in a saucepan with a very little salted water and simmer for ten minutes. Drain off the water; pour over the onions a small cupful of beef stock and cook for ten minutes longer. With a split spoon remove the onions to a hot dish, while you thicken the gravy left in the pan with a heaping teaspoonful of browned flour rubbed to a paste in the same quantity of butter. When you have a smooth brown sauce season it with a teaspoonful, each, of kitchen bouquet and tomato catsup, and salt and pepper to taste. Pour this sauce over the onions.

Stuffed onions, creamed

Boil eight large onions gently until quite tender, but not broken. Drain, and when cold, carefully remove the hearts or centers. Chop three of these hearts fine and mix with them a cupful of minced ham and season to taste. Moisten with rich cream and the beaten yolk of an egg. Fill the centers of the onions with the mixture, put a piece of butter in the top of each, set side by side, in a deep dish, pour a little milk about them and bake, covered, for twenty minutes. Then uncover, sprinkle with buttered crumbs and bake ten minutes longer. Serve hot.

Scalloped onions

Parboil onions and drain. When cold, cut into bits. Put a thick layer of these in the bottom of a greased pudding-dish, sprinkle with salt and pepper and dot with bits of butter. Cover with a very thin layer of crumbs moistened with milk. Put in more seasoned onions and more crumbs, and proceed in this way until the dish is full. Then pour in carefully a little cream, cover and bake for half an hour; uncover and brown.

Onion custard

Cook the onions tender in two waters; drain, and lay in a deep pudding-dish. Thicken a pint of hot milk with a teaspoonful of corn-starch rubbed into two teaspoonfuls of butter and gradually pour this white sauce upon two beaten eggs. Season with pepper and salt and pour the mixture about the onions. Bake until the custard is set.

GREEN PEAS

They lose sweetness with every hour—I might say with every minute—that passes after they have been picked. The passage from garden to kitchen and from pod to pot should be made as short as possible. As you shell throw them into cold water, not holding them in the hand until they are heated and moist. As soon as the last is shelled, drain and cook.

Boiled green peas

Shell and lay in cold water for ten minutes. Drain, turn into slightly salted boiling water and cook for about twenty-five minutes, or until very tender, but not broken. Drain in a colander, put into a dish, stir into the peas a lump of butter, and sprinkle very lightly with salt and pepper.

Green pea pancakes

Boil a pint of shelled peas, and mash while hot, adding a tablespoonful of butter and salt and pepper to taste. Now beat in two whipped eggs, a half pint of milk and five tablespoonfuls of prepared flour. Beat hard and fry on a hot griddle. A soapstone griddle is best. Then they are baked—not fried.

Green pea soufflé

Boil a pint of shelled peas until very tender, and mash with two tablespoonfuls of melted butter. Beat three eggs light and stir into them a pint of milk and the mashed peas. Season with salt and pepper, beat hard and turn into a greased pudding-dish. Bake, covered, for twenty minutes; uncover and brown. Serve this soufflé as soon as it is removed from the oven.

Green pea fritters

Shell enough peas to make a quart without the pods. Lay the peas in cold water for a half hour; put over the fire in two quarts of boiling salted water and cook for half an hour, or until very tender, but not broken. Drain free of water, turn into a bowl and mash soft with two tablespoonfuls of butter and with salt to taste. Beat four eggs very light, add to them three gills of milk and a cupful of flour with which has been sifted a teaspoonful of baking-powder and a half teaspoonful of salt. Stir the mashed peas by the great spoonful into this mixture and beat until you have a smooth, light green batter. Have your soapstone griddle very hot and drop your batter by the spoonful upon this. When done on one side turn and bake to a delicate brown. Serve very hot as a vegetable to accompany any kind of meat or poultry.

TOAST AND ANCHOVIES GARNISHED WITH LEMON
STUFFED TOMATOES GARNISHED WITH RICE AND SHREDDED LEMON
GREEN PEAS GARNISHED WITH POTATOES

Green pea croquettes

Peas that are getting hard will do for these. Boil in just enough salted water to cover them well. While hot, run through the vegetable press. Beat to a smooth paste with a tablespoonful of butter and two of flour. Pepper and salt to taste, drop in a dash of onion juice; lastly, beat in a well-whipped egg. Stir in a vessel set within another of boiling water until hot all through, and set away until cold and stiff. Mold then into croquettes, dip in beaten egg and cracker-crumbs; leave on ice for half an hour before frying in boiling deep cottolene or other fat. Drain and serve very hot.

You may use canned peas if you can not get fresh.

PEPPERS

The large, green peppers, known to the green-grocer as "sweet peppers," have grown rapidly into favor as a fresh vegetable, within the last decade. They must be seeded with the utmost care. A touch of the seeds against the green sides will ruin the latter for present use. Get hold of the inner stem and draw the clustered seeds through the opening at the stem end, without touching the inside walls.

Fried green peppers

Cut open lengthwise and extract all seeds and tough white fiber. Slice crosswise. Lay in cold salted water for ten minutes, then wipe dry. Melt four tablespoonfuls of butter in a frying-pan and sauté the sliced peppers in this. Lay about broiled steak or chops.

Stuffed peppers

Make a forcemeat of a tablespoonful of minced ham, one of minced chicken, three chopped mushrooms and a cupful of boiled rice. Make this paste wet by adding to it a chopped tomato and enough melted butter to make it of the right consistency for stuffing. Smooth the stem-ends, cut the blossom-ends from green peppers and take out the seeds and inside fibers. Lay the green shells for three minutes in salted boiling water, then plunge into iced water. Let them lie in this for fifteen minutes. Drain and wipe dry. Fill with the forcemeat, replace the tips, and stand the peppers, side by side, in a dripping-pan containing a quarter of an inch of soup stock. Cook for twenty minutes, basting twice with a little salad oil. When done, stand the peppers on a platter and pour a little salad oil about them.

Peppers stuffed with fish

Trim the stem-ends of your green peppers so that they will stand up. Cut off the tips and, with a small keen knife, extract the seeds and as much of the tough fiber as will come away. Mince white fish fine, moisten it with a white sauce, season and fill the peppers with this mixture. Stand in the oven long enough to heat through, and serve.

Scalloped peppers au gratin

Cut large green peppers in half, lengthwise, extract core and seeds and fill them with minced cold cooked fish, well seasoned, mixed with one-third its weight of fine bread crumbs. The mixture (forcemeat) must be wet with gravy or tomato sauce. Round the contents of the halved pepper in the shape of the missing other half, sprinkle with fine crumbs, and bake to a light brown.

You may use for these scallops of cold chicken, lean lamb or veal. See that you do not get the forcemeat too stiff.

Scalloped peppers on the half-shell

Halve the peppers lengthwise, remove seeds and membrane, and parboil for five minutes. When cold, fill the halves with minced roast beef and fine bread-crumbs moistened with tomato juice. Bake in a covered pan, basting every ten minutes. At the end of a half hour remove to a hot platter and serve with tomato sauce poured over and around the halved peppers.

Peppers and rice

(A Creole dish.)

Cook half a cupful of rice in plenty of boiling water, a little salt, for twenty minutes hard. Drain in a colander and set at the back of the range to dry off. Heap within a deep dish.

Prepare your peppers as already directed. Slice as for frying in the usual way. When you take them from the cold salt and water, fry them in a great spoonful of butter. Lift them from the pan and chop rather coarsely. Add to the hot butter and peppers a teaspoonful of onion juice and two tablespoonfuls of stock. Boil up and pour upon the rice. Set in the oven, covered, for three minutes, and serve.

POKE STALKS

Cut as you would asparagus, when they are but a few inches high. They are then tender and succulent, and are thought by some imaginative vegetarians to resemble the "aristocrat" in flavor.

They are undeniably wholesome—also inexpensive.

Scrape the stalks and lay in cold water for an hour. Tie loosely together with a piece of soft twine, put over the fire with enough salted water to cover them, and boil until tender. Drain, sprinkle lightly with salt and pepper and lay upon a platter on slices of buttered toast. Pour white sauce over all.

POTATOES

"The Tyrant Potato" is not assailed ignorantly, nor yet flippantly. After careful study of its properties, its works and its ways, the utmost concession that is now made to peculiar prejudice is in the declaration that, since people *will* make potatoes nine-tenths of their vegetable diet, it is essential to the national digestion that the ninety-three parts of water and of starch contained in the tuber be cooked in such manner as shall render the esculent as palatable and as little hurtful as is practicable when the constituents are not to be ignored.

The above protest stands at the head of that section of the "National Cook Book" which is headed "Potatoes." I wrote it ten years ago, and am "of the same opinion still."

Talk against it as we may, the potato holds its sway in defiance of chemistry and dietetics, and our Johns, one and all, insist upon its daily appearance. As one weary housewife said to me:

"If I give my fingers to be burned in the preparation of a half dozen vegetables and have not potatoes in the number, my culinary and housekeeping skill are as sounding brass and tinkling cymbals—to my husband, at least. And I am so tired of the same old ways of cooking the same old potatoes!"

Her remark made me wonder why housekeepers adhere to the "same old ways." Why not try new ones?

One hint may be acted upon with advantage to cook and to eaters.

One of the bugbears to the housewife is paring potatoes. It is not a pleasant task, and the necessity of performing it recurs with disagreeable frequency.

The housekeeper is wise if, while the potatoes are in the process of peeling, she pares and cooks more than enough for the repast for which they are intended, and by utilizing the cold left-overs does away with the necessity of peeling more of the tyrannical starch-and-water for the next meal.

A majority of the recipes herewith given are based upon the supposition that she has done this.

New potatoes with cream sauce

(Contributed)

Boil the potatoes in salted water until done. Drain and cover with a white sauce made as follows: Put two tablespoonfuls of butter into a saucepan and when it begins to bubble add two tablespoonfuls of flour; let them cook for one minute, then add one pint of hot milk, season with salt and pepper and a half teaspoonful of chopped parsley.

Potatoes, boiled au natural

Wash, drop into boiling water slightly salted, and cook fast until a fork will pass easily into the largest. Turn off the water, throw in a handful of salt, and set the pot, uncovered, at the back or side of the range, to dry the potatoes "off." Serve in their skins.

Boiled potatoes

Pare with a sharp knife, and as thin as possible. Much of the mealiness of the potato depends upon this. The scullion who slashes away chunks of her beloved edible really deprives it of its chief merit, and all its comeliness. Have a pot of boiling water ready, salt it slightly and boil fast until a fork pierces the largest readily. Throw off the water immediately, sprinkle with salt, and dry out as directed in last recipe.

Baked potatoes (No. 1)

Select fine potatoes of uniform size. Wash, wipe and bake until the largest yields to the pressure of thumb and finger. Serve wrapped in a hot napkin. If the eater will knead his potato skilfully between his fingers before breaking it open, he will find a mealy mass upon opening it. Never cut a baked potato. It makes it "soggy."

Baked potatoes (No. 2)

Pare and parboil; then set in an open bakepan in the oven and bake about half an hour, basting freely with butter or dripping until you have a delicate brown "glaze" upon each.

These may be eaten as a separate dish, or as a garnish for roast beef.

Stuffed potatoes

Bake eight large potatoes until done. Cut off the tops with a sharp knife and scoop out the insides with a small spoon. Set aside the skins for future use. With the back of a spoon mash the potatoes smooth, rub into them two tablespoonfuls of butter, a gill of cream, two teaspoonfuls of finely minced onion, a teaspoonful of minced parsley and salt and cayenne pepper to taste. When you have worked these ingredients to a smooth mass, beat in the stiffened whites of two eggs. Fill the empty potato skins with this creamy mixture, heaping it high. Stand the potato cases on end, side by side, in a baking-pan and set in the oven until the potato protruding from the tops is a delicate brown.

Potatoes on the half-shell

Bake large smooth potatoes, and cut each carefully in half lengthwise. Scrape out the insides, leaving the skins whole. Beat what you have taken out to a cream with melted butter, cream or milk, season with pepper and salt, and fill the "shells," rounding the potato on top. Put a dot of butter upon each and brown lightly upon the upper grating of your oven.

Potato soufflé

Into two cupfuls of mashed potato work three cupfuls of hot milk in which two tablespoonfuls of butter have been half melted. Beat out all the lumps until you have a smooth purée. Season with salt and pepper. Beat four eggs very light and whip them into the potato and milk. When thoroughly mixed pour into a deep greased pudding-dish and bake in a good oven until "set" and delicately browned.

Potato croquettes

Warm in a double boiler two cupfuls of mashed potatoes and stir into this two teaspoonfuls of butter and the beaten yolks of two eggs. Add enough milk to make the paste of the right consistency to handle easily. With lightly floured hands form into croquettes and set aside to cool. When cold, dip in beaten egg and roll in cracker-dust. Set in the ice-box for several hours longer and fry in deep cottolene or other fat.

Potato fritters

Peel and boil four large potatoes, and when they are cold cut into tiny bits. Make a batter of two eggs—beaten light—a cupful of milk and a cupful and one-half of flour sifted twice with a half teaspoonful of baking-powder. Now add the minced potatoes, mix well and season with salt. Drop this mixture by the spoonful into deep, boiling cottolene or other fat. When the fritters are done lift them out with a perforated spoon, and lay them in a hot colander to drain free of fat.

Scalloped potatoes

Put a layer of sliced cold-boiled potatoes in the bottom of a buttered pudding-dish, sprinkle with crumbs and bits of butter. Put in another layer of potatoes and more crumbs until the dish is full, having the topmost layer of the buttered crumbs. Moisten all by pouring carefully into the dish a cupful of well-seasoned white stock. Bake for twenty minutes.

Stewed potatoes (No. 1)

Peel, cut into neat, *small* dice and lay in cold water for an hour. Put over the fire in boiling water, slightly salted, and cook tender. Turn off the water and pour in a large cupful of hot milk, in which you have stirred a pinch of soda. Boil one minute and stir in a tablespoonful of butter rubbed into one of flour. Pepper and salt, add a tablespoonful of onion juice and a tablespoonful of minced parsley. Simmer for another minute, and serve.

Stewed potatoes (No. 2)

Peel potatoes and cut them into neat squares. Lay in cold water for an hour, drain, and put them over the fire in salted boiling water. Stew until they are tender, but not soft. Turn into a colander to drain. Cook together in a saucepan a heaping teaspoonful, each, of butter and browned flour, and pour upon them a pint of weak beef stock. When you have a smooth, thick sauce, season with pepper, salt and a little onion juice, and mix with the potato dice.

Hashed and browned potatoes

Pare, cut *very* small and evenly, and put into a saucepan with a finely minced onion and a stalk of celery chopped into tiny bits. Cover with salted boiling water and cook tender. Drain off the water, supplying its place with milk, heated with a pinch of soda. Bring to a bubble and stir in a large tablespoonful of butter, rubbed to a cream with one of flour. Pepper, salt, mix well—but taking care not to break the potatoes—take from the fire, stir and toss for a moment, then turn all into a greased pudding-dish, sprinkle crumbs on the top and brown in a good oven.

Potatoes á la duchesse

Peel and boil enough potatoes to make a pint when mashed. Mix with them the yolk of an egg, two tablespoonfuls of melted butter and the same quantity of cream. Turn this mixture upon a pastry-board and press it flat and smooth. With a sharp knife cut the potato paste into squares of uniform size. Slip a cake-turner under each square and transfer it carefully to a greased baking-pan. Set in a cold place to stiffen, then sprinkle with grated Parmesan cheese, and bake in a quick oven to a delicate brown.

Potatoes á la Lyonnaise

Cut cold boiled potatoes into tiny dice of uniform size. Put two great spoonfuls of butter into the frying-pan and fry two sliced onions in this for three minutes. With a skimmer remove the onions and turn the potatoes into the hissing butter. Toss and stir with a fork that the dice may not become brown. When hot, add a teaspoonful of finely chopped parsley and cook a minute longer. Remove the potatoes from the pan with a perforated spoon, that the fat may drip from them. Serve very hot.

Savory potatoes

Heat in a double boiler a quart of milk and put into it three sliced onions. Boil for ten minutes, strain out the onions, return the milk to the fire, and stir into it two teaspoonfuls of butter rubbed into two of flour, and two teaspoonfuls of minced parsley. When the milk is as thick as cream, add to it two cupfuls of sliced cold boiled potatoes. Season with pepper and salt, and as soon as the potatoes are hot, pour all into a greased pudding-dish, sprinkle bread-crumbs over the top and bake until brown.

Potatoes and corn

(A "left-over.")

Cut the kernels from six ears of boiled corn. Cut eight cold boiled potatoes into small dice of uniform size. Put into a frying-pan a tablespoonful of butter and turn the potatoes and corn into this; salt and pepper. Fry, tossing and stirring constantly, for ten minutes.

Fried potato hash

Chop cold boiled potatoes, season with salt, pepper and onion juice. Have two tablespoonfuls of good dripping, hissing hot, in a frying-pan; put in the potatoes and pat smooth. Cook slowly, turning the frying-pan occasionally that they may brown evenly on the bottom. In about twenty minutes they should be nicely colored and crusted into a thick sheet. Reverse carefully upon a hot platter.

Brown creamed potatoes

Cut eight potatoes into small dice of uniform size, boil tender in salted water, drain and stir into a pint of milk which has been thickened with a tablespoonful of flour rubbed into one of butter; season. Turn all into a deep dish and bake until brown.

Potatoes with cheese sauce

Boil a dozen potatoes and, while hot, mash soft with hot milk and melted butter, adding salt and white pepper to taste. Whip light and heap in the center of a fire-proof platter. Smooth the sides of the mound with a knife and carefully remove about a cupful of potato from the center of the mound, leaving a cavity in its place. Dip a feather or brush in the beaten white of an egg and wash the inside of the hollow and the top and sides of the mound with this. Now set in the oven to get very hot and to brown lightly. When done draw to the door of the oven and fill the hollow with the sauce—made according to the following recipe—sprinkle the potatoes and cheese with crumbs and return to the oven for five minutes before sending to the table.

Sauce for the above

Heat a cupful of milk with a generous pinch of soda; season with pepper, salt and onion juice, and thicken with a heaping tablespoonful of butter cooked to a roux with one of flour; cook one minute and add three large spoonfuls of grated Parmesan cheese.

Mashed potatoes

Boil and mash white potatoes and whip to a cream with a cupful of hot milk and a tablespoonful of melted butter. Whip for fully five minutes with two forks, then pile upon a hot platter.

Potato hillock

Boil potatoes, dry at the back of the range, salting well, and rub through a vegetable press or colander upon a fire-proof platter. As they fall let them form a conical hillock in the middle of the platter. Grate cheese thickly over the hillock and brown lightly upon the upper grating of your oven.

Potatoes Parisienne

Parisienne potatoes are cut into small balls from raw potatoes with a French vegetable cutter or a round spoon. They may be either fried, or boiled and served with maître d'hôtel sauce.

French fried potatoes

Peel potatoes, cut into strips, and lay in iced water for at least an hour. Drain and pat dry between the folds of a clean dish-towel that should absorb every drop of moisture. Have ready a kettle of deep cottolene or other fat, heated gradually until it is boiling hot. Test this by dropping in a bit of the potato. It should rise to the top and brown immediately. Put in the potatoes, fry to a golden brown, drain, first in a hot colander, then shake in heated tissue paper before transferring to a hot dish lined with a napkin.

Saratoga chips

Peel the potatoes and proceed as directed in preceding recipe when you have cut them into slices as thin as shavings.

Potatoes au gratin

Slice potatoes thin and put in layers in a greased pudding-dish, sprinkling each layer with salt, pepper and bits of butter. When all are in, pour in a gill of hot water or hot milk, and sprinkle the top layer of potatoes thickly with cracker-crumbs mixed with salt and pepper and bits of butter. Bake, covered, for half an hour. Uncover and brown.

Potato omelet

Make an omelet in the usual way; have ready by the time it is done, and lay upon it, this mixture, then fold down:

Cook one small minced onion in one tablespoonful of dripping until yellow, add one cupful of cold boiled potatoes, chopped fine, and cook until slightly colored, stirring frequently. Shake into it a little pepper and salt and one teaspoonful of finely minced parsley.

Set into the oven to keep warm until the omelet is ready.

Potato dumplings (No. 1)

Grate ten or twelve large raw potatoes. Put the grated pulp into a muslin bag and press out the juice. Turn into a bowl and add one-third as much boiled potato that has been run through a vegetable press. Salt to taste and beat in a raw egg until you have a smooth, creamy paste. Make into dumplings with well-floured hands, and roll each in flour to prevent them from sticking together while they are boiling.

Have a pot of water at a hard boil, drop in the dumplings and cook from ten to twelve minutes. Test by taking one out and cutting in two to see if it is done in the center. Take up with a skimmer and serve at once, as they soon get heavy.

Serve them with any kind of roast meat, or alone with gravy.

Potato dumplings (No. 2)

Peel medium-sized potatoes that have been partly boiled (not quite soft). When cold, grate; to three parts of the potatoes take one part of grated wheat bread, and add small squares of wheat bread browned in butter, then crushed into crumbs.

To each pint of the above add two eggs, well-beaten, two ounces of melted butter and nutmeg to suit taste. Mix all thoroughly and form into round dumplings the size of an egg, or larger, as preferred. Roll in flour and boil in salted water until dry inside, or about fifteen minutes.

Serve with roast meats.

Always use mealy potatoes.

Potato balls ("Kartoffelklösse")

(A German recipe.)

Peel, boil and mash potatoes; put aside to cool.

Three cupfuls of potatoes, one cupful of bread, two eggs, well-beaten, separately; pepper, salt and nutmeg to taste, and some chopped parsley that has been heated in butter. The bread should be prepared as for croutons, crusts removed, cut in squares, browned in butter in the oven, then crushed. The mixture should be very stiff. Mold into small balls and drop into boiling, well-salted water; keep water boiling for fifteen minutes, when the klösse should be about twice the original size and done to the cen ter. They may be served with bread-crumbs browned in butter, placed on the top of each dumpling, or with tomato sauce. With chopped meat filling the center of the dumplings they can also be varied. If too moist, use flour or bread-crumbs in molding. A good cook has the knack of dropping from the spoon without molding, but this is hard to do. The klösse should be the size of small apples when finished. Americans very often use a trifle of baking-powder to insure lightness in these. Germans depend on good beating.

SWEET POTATOES

Boiled sweet potatoes

Wash and cook in boiling water until soft. Set in a moderate oven for ten minutes to keep them from being watery.

Baked sweet potatoes

They are seldom cooked in any other way at the South, where they are native to the soil, and at their best estate.

Wash and wipe and bake in a good oven until tender.

Glazed sweet potatoes

Parboil in their skins, peel and lay in a bake-pan. Cook, basting often with butter, until they are a golden brown.

Scallop of sweet potatoes and bacon

This is a good "left-over" when you have a little cold corned ham and some cold boiled or baked sweet potatoes. Mince the meat—the fatter the better—and put a layer in the bottom of a bake-dish. Cover with sweet potato dice, pepper, and put in more bacon. When all the materials are used up, cover with crumbs; add enough milk to wet the crumbs, cover and bake half an hour. Uncover and brown.

Sweet potatoes au gratin

Parboil the potatoes, peel and slice while hot. Butter a deep dish well; put in a layer of potatoes, sprinkle with sugar, salt, pepper, and dot with butter; then a stratum of fine crumbs; season in the same way, leaving out the sugar. The uppermost layer should be of crumbs and well buttered. Pour in four tablespoonfuls of warm water to generate steam, cover closely and bake half an hour. Uncover and brown.

This is an especially nice dish for a family dinner, and always liked by children.

Buttered sweet potatoes

Boil sweet potatoes and peel them. Lay in a deep dish and upon each potato put a teaspoonful of butter. Set in the oven and heat until the butter sizzles about the edge of the dish. Then send to the table.

Sweet potato croquettes

Into two cupfuls of boiled and mashed sweet potatoes beat a tablespoonful of butter, and stir in a saucepan over the fire until smoking hot. Now remove and add a tablespoonful of cream and the yolks of two eggs. When cold, form into croquettes and roll each croquette in beaten egg and cracker-crumbs. Arrange all on a platter and set in a cold place for several hours before frying in deep cottolene or other fat to a golden brown.

Sweet potato puff

Into two cupfuls of boiled and mashed sweet potatoes beat three whipped eggs, a cupful of milk, two tablespoonfuls of melted butter and seasoning to taste. Beat hard and bake in a greased pudding-dish.

Sweet potato and chestnut croquettes

Boil and mash enough sweet potatoes to make two cupfuls, and enough Spanish chestnuts to make one cupful. Rub the nuts and potatoes together while hot and beat into them two tablespoonfuls of butter, four teaspoonfuls of cream, two beaten eggs, and season to taste. When cold, form into croquettes, roll in egg and cracker-crumbs, and set in a cold place for an hour before frying in deep, boiling cottolene or other fat.

RICE

Boiled rice

Into three pints of hot salted water, when at a fast boil, throw half a cupful of raw rice, previously washed and picked over. Keep it at a furious boil for twenty minutes, when test a grain to see if it is done. If it is soft, drain away every drop of water; set the uncovered pot at the back of the range for two minutes to dry off the rice, and serve. Not a spoon should touch it while cooking, and each grain should be whole and apart from the rest.

This, the one and only way to boil rice properly, is also the easiest. Shake the saucepan up three times while the rice is in cooking, to make sure it does not clog.

Pasty rice is as abhorrent to those who have eaten it cooked according to this recipe as sodden, gluey potatoes.

Serve in a hot, uncovered dish. Eat with butter, salt and pepper, and you will not regret the tyrant potato, should he fail to appear.

Buttered rice

Spread three cups of cold boiled rice upon a platter and set in the open oven that every grain may dry. Meanwhile, heat a little butter in the frying-pan and fry a sliced onion in it. When the slices are browned remove them with a perforated spoon, and lay the rice by the spoonful in the pan. Stir until each grain is coated with the butter; turn the rice into a heated colander, shake hard, and set at the side of the range for five minutes. Serve in a deep vegetable dish.

Rice croquettes

Boil as directed in first recipe; drain, and beat in two whipped eggs, half a cupful of milk (or cream if you have it), a little butter, a teaspoonful of sugar, a little mace, pepper and salt. Set by until perfectly cold, form into croquettes, roll in egg and fine crumbs, leave on ice for an hour and fry in boiling deep cottolene or other fat.

You can make the croquettes of cold boiled rice if you have it, but it is hardly as good for the purpose as the hot. The croquettes seldom have the consistency of those made up while the rice is hot.

Rice and tomato croquettes

When the rice has boiled ten minutes drain off the water and cover the rice with tomato juice, already heated and seasoned with pepper, salt and sugar. Cook ten minutes more, or until the rice is tender. Take from the fire, add a great spoonful of butter and a teaspoonful of onion juice; the beaten yolks of three eggs, and, when you have beaten these in, two tablespoonfuls of grated Parmesan cheese. Set in a pan of boiling water and stir over the fire for five minutes. Turn out and let it get perfectly cold. Make into croquettes, roll in egg and cracker crumbs; set on ice for an hour and fry in hot, deep cottolene or other fat. Drain and serve.

Boiled rice with tomato sauce

Boil in the usual way, dish, and pour over it, loosening with a fork that the sauce may penetrate to every part, a generous cupful of rich tomato sauce, seasoned with pepper, salt, onion juice and sugar, and, finally, with two tablespoonfuls of grated cheese.

Savory rice

Prepare as in last recipe, but add a small cupful of good stock to an equal quantity of tomato sauce; cook together for two minutes and pour over the rice.

Rice pudding as a vegetable

Boil one cupful of raw rice twenty minutes, or until soft, but not broken. Beat four eggs light, and when you have stirred a tablespoonful of butter into the rice add these and season with pepper and salt. Stir in, gradually, a scant quart of milk; beat all well for one minute, turn into a buttered pudding-dish and bake, covered, half an hour; then brown.

It should be as light as a soufflé, and must be eaten at once. A pleasing accompaniment to roast poultry of any kind.

Savory rice pudding

Boil and drain a cupful of rice. Stir into it, while hot, a tablespoonful of butter and a cupful of hot milk with which has been mixed a teaspoonful of corn-starch dissolved in cold water. Add a well-beaten egg, salt and pepper, and spread upon a platter to cool. Meanwhile make ready two cupfuls of chopped meat of almost any kind—poultry, veal, lamb, mutton, beef, giblets, liver—or a mixture of several—whatever you have on hand. Chop half a can of mushrooms and work in; season highly with paprika, kitchen bouquet and onion juice. Some even put in a little curry. Moisten slightly with gravy and when the rice has cooled mix all well together. Butter a cake mold lavishly, put the pudding into it; fit on a close top and set in a pot of boiling water. Cook steadily for at least two hours. Dip the mold into ice-water to loosen the pudding from the sides, and turn out upon a hot platter.

Send tomato sauce, mixed with grated cheese, around with it, or any gravy you may chance to have left over.

Molded rice (No. 1)

Boil a cupful of raw rice ten minutes; drain and pour over it, in place of the water, two cupfuls of chicken gravy or stock made from chicken, duck or turkey bones, seasoned well with salt, pepper and onion juice. Set in boiling water uncovered, and cook gently until quite dry. Turn into a bowl wet with hot water, press down firmly and reverse the bowl upon a hot platter. Cover the mound with grated cheese, brush all over with beaten white of egg, sift grated cheese upon the egg, and set upon the top grating of your oven to color slightly.

Molded rice (No. 2)

Boil a cupful of rice in plenty of hot salted water until soft. Drain and dry off. Stir into it a great spoonful of butter, a teaspoonful of onion juice and the beaten yolks of two eggs, with salt and pepper to taste. Stir over the fire in a bowl set in boiling water for two minutes, using a fork that you may not break the rice to pieces. Turn into a round-bottomed bowl wet with cold water, and press down hard. Reverse the bowl upon a fireproof platter, cover the molded rice thickly with a meringue made of the whites of the eggs beaten stiff, and set upon the top grating of the oven for three minutes to form.

Eat with drawn butter.

Spanish rice (very nice)

Boil one cupful of rice until tender in plenty of boiling water, salted; drain and dry off. Chop a quarter of a pound of fat salt pork, and fry in a pan. When it hisses put into the pan two medium-sized onions, also minced. Chop two green sweet peppers (seeded, of course), and mix with the rice, then the pork and onions, and enough tomato sauce to moisten the mixture well. Butter a bake-dish, add salt and pepper, if needed, to the rice, and put into the dish. Coat thickly with fine crumbs and bake, covered, for twenty minutes; then brown.

Rice timbales

Pack hot boiled rice in slightly buttered timbale molds; let them stand in hot water for ten minutes; run a pointed knife around the sides; turn from the molds and serve as a garnish for curried meats or boiled fowl.

SALSIFY, OR OYSTER-PLANT

Stewed salsify

Scrape the roots, throwing them at once into cold water, that they may not blacken. Cut into inch lengths and put over the fire in boiling salted water. Stew until tender. Drain off the water and pour upon the salsify in the saucepan a cup of hot milk. After it has simmered five minutes add a tablespoonful of butter and three tablespoonfuls of cracker dust; season to taste and serve.

Mock fried oysters

Wash, trim and cook a bunch of oyster-plant (or salsify) in boiling salted water until tender. Drain and scrape off the skin. Mash well, and if stringy rub through a colander.

To one pint of the mashed salsify add one teaspoonful of flour, one tablespoonful of butter, one well-beaten egg, and salt and pepper to season highly. Take up a small spoonful and shape it into an oval about the size of a large oyster; dip each lightly in flour or very fine cracker crumbs, and brown on each side in hot butter.

Salsify fritters

Scrape the salsify and grate it fine. If you have a machine for grinding vegetables, use that, as the process of grinding is so rapid that there is not time for the salsify to discolor before it is prepared. Have made a batter of two beaten eggs, half a cupful of flour, a gill of milk, and salt to taste. Beat hard, and whip the grated salsify into this. Drop by the spoonful into deep, boiling cottolene or other fat. When the fritters are of the right shade of brown, drain them quickly in a hot colander to free them of superfluous grease. Serve very hot.

Scalloped salsify

Wash and trim, but do not scrape fine roots of salsify. Boil in salted water until tender. Drain, scrape, clean and cut into inch lengths. Pack into a buttered bake-dish, alternately with thick white drawn butter, well seasoned, and fine bread-crumbs, seasoned and buttered. The top layer should be crumbs wet with cream. Cover closely and bake half an hour; then brown delicately.

Not a bad imitation of scalloped oysters.

SPINACH

"Spinach is one of our most valuable vegetables. It contains salts and is slightly laxative. In order to retain all the nutritive value and the salts in the spinach it is best to cook in a steamer. It should be cooked just long enough to be tender, which is from ten to fifteen minutes. Spinach, if cooked too long, will lose its flavor and color."

Thus writes an able authority upon dietetics. In three sentences we have here condensed the cardinal rules for preparing this queenly esculent for the use of the human animal. Opposed to one clause of the summary we have the story of a noted epicure who found spinach so much better when warmed up for the thirteenth time that he ordered his cook to cook it thirteen times on the first day of serving.

Boiled spinach, plain

Pick over the spinach, rejecting all yellow or dried leaves. Wash in four waters, letting it soak in the last cold bath for three-quarters of an hour. Put into a large pot over the fire with just enough cold water to cover it. Cook for twenty minutes, or until tender. Drain in a colander, then turn into a wooden chopping-bowl and chop very, *very* fine. Return the spinach to the saucepan, stir into it a great spoonful of butter, and salt and pepper to taste. Mound the spinach on a hot platter, and garnish with slices of hard-boiled eggs.

Spinach á la crême

Pick over and wash the spinach as in the last recipe. After soaking in the fourth water, put the leaves, with the moisture still clinging to them, into a large pot, and cover closely. The moisture on the leaves and the juice of the vegetables will form enough liquor to prevent scorching. Cook for twenty minutes, stirring well several times during the process. Sprinkle with salt and turn into a colander to drain. Press out the liquid, turn the spinach into a chopping-bowl and chop as fine as possible. Cook together in a saucepan one tablespoonful of flour and two of butter, and, when they are blended, pour the spinach upon them. Season and cook for several minutes, stirring constantly. Pour upon the spinach a small cupful of cream in which a pinch of soda has been dissolved, and cook three minutes longer, still stirring. Now add pepper and salt to taste and a pinch of nutmeg, and beat hard for three minutes. Serve smoking-hot, garnished with small triangles of toast.

Spinach puff

Boil as in the former recipe, chop "exceeding small," and beat in a tablespoonful of melted butter, salt, pepper and a pinch of nutmeg. Set aside until cool, then stir in a gill of cream, the whipped yolks of two eggs and the stiffened whites of three. Beat hard and turn into a deep, greased pudding-dish. Bake for twenty minutes, and serve at once.

Spinach soufflé

Boil the spinach and chop fine. Add the beaten yolks of two eggs, a tablespoonful of melted butter, salt and pepper to taste. Set this mixture away to cool. When cold, beat into it a half-gill of cream and the frothed whites of three eggs. Turn into a buttered pudding-dish, and bake quickly in a hot oven to a light brown. Serve as soon as it is removed from the oven.

Spinach pátés

Boil the spinach, press out every drop of water and chop fine. Cook together in a saucepan a tablespoonful of butter and two of flour. Add the spinach with pepper and salt to taste; cook for five minutes. Butter the insides of muffin-tins or pâté-pans, and press the spinach hard into these. Set in the oven to keep hot while you make a white sauce. Carefully turn out the forms of spinach on a hot platter, lay a slice of hard-boiled egg on the top of each form and pour the white sauce around it.

SQUASH

The summer squash differs from the winter variety in having a tender shell and in being very juicy. Both may be cooked in a variety of ways, and form many appetizing dishes. In opening the winter squash it is often necessary to exert great strength to break through the outer rind—some housekeepers using a small saw for the purpose. The summer vegetable may be easily peeled or sliced with an ordinary case-knife.

Boiled squash

Wash two summer squashes, pare them, and cut into pieces about an inch square. Put them over the fire in a saucepan of boiling water and boil steadily for twenty-five minutes. Drain in a colander, pressing hard to extract the water, turn into a wooden bowl and mash with a potato-beater until free from lumps. Now beat in a heaping tablespoonful of butter; salt and pepper to taste. Return to the fire just long enough to get very hot, stirring all the time. Serve in a deep vegetable dish.

Baked squash

Peel, boil and mash two small squashes. When cold, beat in two tablespoonfuls of melted butter, two whipped eggs, a gill of cream and salt and pepper to taste. Turn into a greased bake dish, sprinkle with bread-crumbs and bake for a half-hour. A good way to use squash left over from yesterday.

Creamed squash

Peel two summer squashes and cut into dice of uniform size. Boil for fifteen minutes in salted water, or until tender, but not broken. Drain carefully in a colander and keep hot while you cook together two heaping teaspoonfuls of butter and the same quantity of flour until they bubble; then pour upon them a cupful and a half of sweet milk. Stir until smooth; turn in the squash dice, season liberally with salt and white pepper, and serve.

Scalloped squash

Peel, wash and boil three summer squashes according to directions given in the recipe for boiled squash. Beat two eggs light, and whip into them a small cupful of rich sweet milk, and a tablespoonful of melted butter. Beat this mixture into the mashed squash, season with salt and pepper and turn all into a greased pudding-dish. Sprinkle with bread-crumbs and bits of butter, and bake.

Squash pancakes

Boil and mash two squashes, and when cold beat into them two tablespoonfuls of melted butter, a quarter of a teaspoonful of salt, a pint of milk, two eggs and a cupful of flour in which has been sifted a teaspoonful of baking-powder. Beat hard for five minutes. Have a soapstone griddle heated, and drop the mixture by the spoonful on this. If the cakes are too stiff, add a little more milk. Serve hot with butter. These are good with broiled steaks or chops.

Squash fritters

Peel and slice the squash, and boil in salted water for a little over five minutes. Carefully remove the slices and drop into iced water. When cold, drain in a colander and pat dry between the folds of a dish-towel. Dip each slice in beaten egg, then in cracker crumbs, and when all are thoroughly coated set in a cold place for an hour. Have ready a kettle of boiling dripping; drop the squash slices carefully into this and fry to a golden brown. Drain in a heated colander, sprinkle with pepper and salt, and serve.

TOMATOES

The nineteenth century was a third gone before the world on this side of the sea began to appreciate the beneficent qualities of what our foremothers used to call "love apples." There is no other vegetable that is of more value as a liver regulator and blood-cooler than the tomato. The small quantity of calomel it contains acts as a corrective of biliousness, and stimulates all the secretions of the body to activity. Eaten raw, it is cooling and delicious, and it may be cooked in so many and varied forms that one does not soon weary of it.

In the average home it appears as a salad, in soup, stewed, and perhaps baked or scalloped. When it has been thus served many housekeepers consider that they have exhausted its capabilities. On the contrary, they have hardly touched upon its possibilities.

The increasing familiarity with sauces as the cook's potent aids in converting old dishes into new, has made tomato sauce popular as an accompaniment of certain compounds of macaroni, but even those who use the sauce in this manner do not all know how admirable it is served with boiled or baked fish, or with roast mutton, or as a vehicle for shrimps, or as a zest for eggs. Apart from this, the tomato, not made into a sauce, but employed either fresh or canned, may come to the table in a variety of easily-prepared and savory combinations that will appeal to the family caterer as being the new and inexpensive dishes she is always seeking.

Raw tomatoes

Never scald them. Pare and strip off the skins. Set on ice until you are ready to serve. Cut up quickly, lay within a chilled bowl and season, as you serve, with French dressing.

Raw tomatoes and cucumbers

Cut off the tops of large, firm tomatoes and carefully remove most of the pulp. Keep pulp and tomatoes in the refrigerator while you peel and cut into small dice ice-cold cucumbers. Mix the cucumber dice with the tomato pulp, fill the tomato shells, set them on crisp lettuce leaves and pour a great spoonful of mayonnaise dressing over each.

Creamed tomatoes

Cut firm tomatoes into thick slices and fry them until tender in a couple of spoonfuls of butter. Have ready a white sauce made by cooking together a tablespoonful, each, of butter and flour to the bubbling point, and then pouring upon them a half-pint of milk—or, better still, a half-pint of mingled milk and cream. Cook, stirring constantly, until the sauce thickens, dish the tomatoes and turn the sauce upon them, after seasoning them suitably with pepper and salt.

Stewed tomatoes

Peel, slice and put a quart of tomatoes over the fire in a nickel-steel-plated or agate saucepan—never in tin. Stew fast twenty minutes. Season with a lump of butter rolled in flour, a teaspoonful of sugar, salt and pepper to taste, and two teaspoonfuls of onion juice. Stew five minutes longer, and serve.

Some cooks substitute fine dry crumbs for the flour. Unless some thickening is used, the tomatoes will be watery and thin.

Raw tomatoes and whipped cream

Pare large, smooth tomatoes carefully, and set on ice until chilled to the heart. Cut each in half when ready to serve, sprinkle lightly with salt and paprika, and heap with whipped cream.

A welcome entrée in summer. Send around heated and but tered crackers and cream cheese with them, or thin slices of buttered graham bread.

Tomato croquettes

These can be made either of fresh or canned tomatoes. Rub through a colander half the contents of a can of tomatoes into a saucepan with a thin slice of onion, salt, pepper, two or three cloves, and one tablespoonful of sugar. Cook for fifteen minutes, thicken with corn-starch—four teaspoonfuls of it rubbed to a cream with a generous lump of butter. Let it boil up and add one egg. Pour the mixture out to cool. When cool, form into croquettes, and dip them, first, in beaten egg, then in fine crumbs; set on ice for two hours before frying in deep, boiling cottolene or other fat.

Stuffed tomatoes (No. 1)

Cut the tops from large, firm tomatoes, and with a small spoon scoop out the insides. To half of this pulp, chopped, add as much minced boiled ham and two tablespoonfuls of bread-crumbs. Season to taste and fill the tomatoes with this mixture. Set in a baking-pan and bake for twenty minutes, covered; then brown.

Stuffed tomatoes (No. 2)

Cut the tops from large tomatoes and scrape out the pulp. Mix with this one part of bread-crumbs to two parts of minced boiled ham. Fill the tomato shells with this mixture, put a bit of butter upon the top of each, and set, side by side, in a bake-pan. Pour a cupful of soup stock over and around the tomatoes, and bake until tender.

Scalloped tomatoes

Grease a pudding-dish and put in the bottom of it a layer of peeled and sliced tomatoes. Cover with a layer of salted and peppered crumbs, sprinkle with bits of butter and a little sugar. Now put in another stratum of tomatoes and more crumbs. When the dish is full pour over all a cupful of well-seasoned soup stock, sprinkle the top with crumbs, and bake, covered, for fifteen minutes. Uncover and brown.

Tomatoes and corn

Put a cupful, each, of stewed tomatoes and boiled corn over the fire together, bring to a boil, add half a teaspoonful of white sugar and, if you like, a dash of onion juice; cook one minute longer and serve.

A good way of using yesterday's left-overs of these vegetables.

Tomato fritters

Make a batter of a cupful of flour, a cupful of water, a tablespoonful of butter, a saltspoonful of salt and the white of an egg. The water should be just warm enough to melt the butter, but not hot. Stir the two into the sifted and salted flour, mixing carefully, and, lastly, beat in the whipped white of an egg. Into the batter thus made dip rather thick slices of peeled tomatoes, and fry in deep hot fat to a light, delicate brown. The tomatoes may be sprinkled with salt and pepper before dipping them in batter, or the fritters may be seasoned after they are cooked.

Tomatoes stuffed with meat

Select large, firm tomatoes, cut off the tops and scoop out the inside pulp. Do not peel. Chop fine a cupful of cold meat—it may be fowl, tongue or ham, or even lamb, mutton or beef, if the latter are well seasoned. With the meat put a half cupful of fine bread-crumbs, a tablespoonful of butter, and salt, pepper, parsley and onion juice. The quantity of these to be used must be determined by the amount of seasoning there is already in the meat. After sprinkling the inside of the tomato shells with a very little salt and pepper fill them with the mixture of meat, crumbs, etc. If this seems too dry it may be moistened with a small quantity of gravy or soup stock, or even with milk or cream. Arrange the tomatoes in a pudding-dish, replace the tops, lay a cover over them and bake half an hour. Serve in the dish in which they were cooked.

Tomatoes stuffed with corn

Prepare the tomatoes as in the preceding recipe, place them in the bake-dish and fill them with a mixture of a cupful of grated green corn, half a cupful of bread-crumbs, a tablespoonful, each, of milk and butter, a teaspoonful of white sugar, and salt and pepper to taste.

Tomatoes stuffed with rice

Fill tomato shells prepared as above directed with cold boiled rice, to which have been added two tablespoonfuls of melted butter, half a teaspoonful of onion juice, salt and paprika. When the shells are filled strew the contents of each thickly with grated cheese before laying on the tops. Bake, covered, half an hour.

Tomatoes stuffed with macaroni

Prepare as in last recipe, substituting cold, boiled macaroni, chopped, for the rice, and mixing cheese with the filling, besides strewing it on the top.

Tomatoes à la créme

Cut unpeeled tomatoes into thick slices. Put into a frying-pan three tablespoonfuls of butter, and fry the tomatoes for three minutes in this, or until they are tender. Remove carefully and keep hot on a platter set in an open oven. Into the butter in the pan stir a tablespoonful of flour and cook until thoroughly blended; then pour in gradually a half-pint of rich milk in which a pinch of soda has been dissolved. Stir all to a smooth sauce, season and pour over the fried tomatoes.

Tomatoes and poached eggs

Cook tomatoes by either of the preceding recipes, or stew them until tender. If you do the latter, strain off the thin, watery liquor that comes from them in cooking, and set it aside for sauces or for seasoning. Make of the thick portion of the to mato a layer in the bottom of a platter, seasoning to taste with pepper and salt, and, if desired, with a few drops of onion juice; make all very hot and lay on the bed thus prepared carefully poached eggs. If fried eggs are preferred, they may be substituted. Dust them with a little salt and pepper and serve at once.

Tomato omelet

Peel and chop four tomatoes. Soak a cupful of bread-crumbs in a cup of milk and stir them into five beaten eggs. Add the chopped tomatoes, season to taste and turn into a frying-pan in which two tablespoonfuls of butter have been melted. Cook until set, turn upon a hot platter, pour tomato sauce about the omelet, and send at once to the table.

Curried tomatoes

Put into a frying-pan a heaping tablespoonful of butter and half a small onion, grated. Cook until the latter begins to brown—about two minutes—and stir in a scant teaspoonful of curry powder. In this fry thick slices of tomato until tender, sprinkle with salt and serve.

Another method of preparing curried tomatoes is to cook them by the recipe given for creamed tomatoes, adding a teaspoonful of curry powder to the cream sauce and pouring this over the fried tomatoes.

Curried green tomatoes

Cut large green tomatoes into very thick slices. Melt in a frying-pan three tablespoonfuls of butter and fry in this a small onion, sliced. At the end of two or three minutes stir into the melted butter a teaspoonful of curry powder. Lay the tomatoes in this mixture and fry them on both sides. When done, drain, sprinkle with salt and pepper, and serve.

TURNIPS

Mashed turnips

Peel, lay in cold water for an hour; boil tender in hot, salted water; throw this off and fill up the pot with boiling water, slightly salted. Cook five minutes in this, drain well and rub through a colander or vegetable-press. Beat in a lump of butter rolled in a little flour, salt and pepper to taste; return to the saucepan and cook one minute, stirring all the time.

Turnips boiled, plain

Pare and quarter. Cook tender in two waters; drain, dish; pour a little melted butter, seasoned with pepper and salt, over them, and serve *hot*.

Young turnips stewed with cream

Pare, lay in cold water one hour; cook tender in two waters; drain and cover with hot cream (heated with a pinch of soda) or hot milk, if you have no cream. Simmer gently for five minutes; stir in a white roux made by cooking together a tablespoonful of butter and one of flour, salt and pepper, and serve very hot.

Young turnips with white sauce

Peel, lay in cold water for an hour; boil for ten minutes in fresh water, cover with boiling, slightly salted water, and cook tender. Drain, dish, season and pour over them a good white sauce of drawn butter.

Fried turnips

Peel and slice young turnips, dropping them into cold water as you do so. Turn into a pot of boiling water, and cook for twenty minutes. Drain carefully, so as not to break the slices. When cold, dip each slice in beaten egg, then in salted cracker dust, and spread all upon a platter. Let them stand for an hour and fry in deep, boiling fat to a golden brown.

Turnips and carrots sautés

Peel and cut into dice of uniform size enough cold boiled turnips and carrots to make a cupful of each. Mix and sprinkle with salt and pepper. Melt two tablespoonfuls of butter in a frying-pan and turn the vegetable dice into this. Toss and turn in the hissing butter for five or ten minutes; drain in a hot colander and dish.

Kohlrabi turnips

Separate the turnip of the vegetable from the leaves that surround it and wash thoroughly. Cut into quarters and boil for twenty minutes in salted water. Drain; sprinkle with salt and pepper, and serve hot with melted butter.

Kohlrabi with leaves

Remove the outer leaves from the swelled stalk, or turnip; wash thoroughly and throw into cold water. Drain both and put them on to boil in separate vessels of salted water. When the turnips have cooked for ten minutes, drain and pour over them fresh boiling water, to which a tablespoonful of vinegar has been added. Boil for ten minutes longer; drain, scrape and slice. Dip the slices, one by one, in melted butter and lay about the edge of a hot platter. Drain the leaves which have been cooked tender, turn into a chopping-bowl and chop very fine. Return to the fire with two tablespoonfuls of butter, pepper and salt to taste. Beat to a smoking mass, and heap in the center of the heated platter, about the edge of which you have laid the sliced vegetable.

A WORD ABOUT NUTS

Nuts of all kinds are gaining in favor as articles of diet, and are at their best in the autumn and winter. They may be bought, shelled and packed in boxes, so that they are ready for immediate use. The housekeeper of moderate means, with an abundance of time at her disposal, will find that it is cheaper to buy the nuts in their shells and crack them herself. If she is so fortunate as to be able to despise the petty economies she will rejoice in the prepared nuts. They will save her much tedious labor.

If Spanish chestnuts are not to be procured when wanted, large domestic chestnuts may be boiled and used in their stead.

Chestnut croquettes

Boil a quart of Spanish chestnuts in salted water. While still hot, remove the shells and skins and rub the nuts through a colander. With a wooden spoon work to a smooth paste, adding, as you do so, a tablespoonful of butter, a saltspoonful of salt, a dash of paprika, a quarter of a teaspoonful of onion juice, a handful of fine bread-crumbs, and the unbeaten yolk of an egg. Put the paste in a double boiler over the fire and heat through. With floured hands form into croquettes, dip in beaten egg, then in cracker dust, and lay on a platter in the refrigerator for two hours. Fry in deep, boiling cottolene or other fat; drain in a colander, and serve very hot.

English walnut croquettes

Crack, extract the kernels, blanch by pouring boiling water over them, stripping off the loosened skins and dropping into cold water. Leave there for ten minutes; take out, dry between two soft towels and, when crisp and perfectly dry, proceed as with chestnuts in last recipe.

Peanut stuffing for roast duck

Prepare the ducks for roasting and make a stuffing of bread-crumbs seasoned with butter, pepper and salt. Chop a cupful of roasted and shelled peanuts to a powder and rub them into the bread-crumbs. Stuff the ducks with this mixture and roast, basting frequently.

Savory chestnuts

Boil and shell and skin large Spanish chestnuts; break each in half and cover with a thin giblet gravy. Or you may make a gravy of the legs and necks of a pair of fowls, and thicken it with browned flour rolled in butter. The gravy must be brown. Cook the chestnuts in it for ten minutes. This is a pleasing accompaniment to roast poultry of any kind, particularly roast turkey.

DINNER SWEETS OF ALL SORTS

PIES

Pastry

Have all ingredients very cold. Into a pound of flour chop three-quarters of a cup of firm, cold butter. When the flour is like a coarse powder stir into it a small cupful of iced water. With a spoon mix together, then turn upon a floured pastry-board, roll out quickly and lightly, fold and roll out again. Set the pastry on the ice until chilled through, roll out and line a pie-dish with it. Before filling the pastry shell with fruit, or other material of which the pie is to be made, wash over the lower crust with the unbeaten white of an egg, and, when the filling is put in, set the pie immediately in an oven that is as hot at the bottom as at the top. The oven must be hot and steady.

A good puff paste

Into a half-pound of flour chop six ounces of firm, cold butter, and, when like a coarse powder, wet with a small cupful of iced water. Stir to a paste and turn upon a chilled board. Roll out quickly and lightly, handling as little as possible. Fold and roll out three times, then set on the ice for several hours before making into pies. Always bake pastry in a very hot oven.

Family pie crust

Sift a quart of flour three times with one teaspoonful of baking-powder. Chop into it two tablespoonfuls of cottolene or other fat until it is like granulated dust. Wet with iced water into a stiff dough, handling as little as you can, using a wooden spoon until it is too stiff to manage. Turn upon a floured board and roll out thin. Have ready two tablespoonfuls of firm butter, and with this dot the paste in rows one inch apart, using one tablespoonful of butter. Roll up the sheet of paste, inclosing the butter; beat flat with the rolling-pin, and roll out as before. Use the other tablespoonful of butter in dotting this sheet, sprinkle lightly with flour, and roll up tightly. Give a blow or two of the pin to hold it in fold, and set on the ice until you are ready to use it—all night if you like. It is better for three or four hours' chilling.

Butter the pie-plates, lay the crust lightly within them; pinch the edges to hinder it from "crawling" while baking, fill with fruit, or whatever else is to go into them. If this is to be what a witty editor designates as "the kivered pie which stands high in the royal family of Pie," lay the paste neatly over the filling, trim off ragged edges, and press or print down the edges.

A North Carolina man thus separates the "royal family" aforesaid: "There are three varieties: kivered, unkivered and barred."

The New York editor, just quoted, says of the "kivered" variety:

"Its triumphant composition requires of the artist higher qualities of head and heart, a more delicate touch, a higher strain of genius, a sublimer imagination, than the composition of the unkivered, or the barred. There must be magic in the upper crust of it. Ah! that delicious, finely-flaking upper crust, designed by a deep-revolving brain and fashioned by a sensitive hand, a pâté Queen Mab would be glad to nibble!"

On the other hand, a New Orleans knight of the pen boldly defines the kivered pie as "distinctively a product of New England civilization, that has no place in simpler and more democratic states. Descendants of the men who made the charge up King's Mountain, the Majuba Hill of this continent, take their pie unkivered. They will not touch the kivered abomination!"

Mince pie

Returning to our New York editorial, the amused reader finds this eulogium upon mince pie:

"There goes much skill to the making of a mince pie. Within the fortunate inwards of the president of pies are strange dainties and spices, and Dr. Johnson's drink of heroes. The elements are so mixed in it that nature may stand up and say to all the world: 'This is a *pie*! A great mince pie is a masterpiece!'"

An anonymous writer upon the same subject says for the comfort of semi-dyspeptics:

"Mince-meat ought to be extremely wholesome for the same reasons that make it good to eat—its flavors of sweet and sour, of meat, apple and spice, which relieve each other, and its finely divided particles which allow the choicer blending of flavors and save the stomach much of the grinding work which reduces food to the pulp in which it enters the blood. What gives mince pie its ill repute as the very spawn of nightmare, are its overdressing with suet and butter, only fit for polar consumption, and its drugging with spices. Spice is the very food of the nerves, rightly used, growing more essential as circulation and sense dull with age. But it should be delicately, discerningly used not to lose its potency. The overdressing with fat is a relic of the old English barbarism which stewed its food in tallow, and, as the old play has it, 'took two fat wethers to baste one capon.'"

Mince-meat

(A family recipe 150 years old.)

Boil two pounds of lean beef, and when cold, chop fine. Mince a pound of beef suet to a powder. Peel and chop five pounds of apples. Seed and halve two pounds of raisins. Wash, and pick over carefully two pounds of cleaned currants and one pound of sultana raisins. Cut into tiny bits three-quarters of a pound of citron. Mix these ingredients, adding, as you do so, two tablespoonfuls, each, of cinnamon and mace, a tablespoonful, each, of cloves and allspice, a teaspoonful of ground nutmeg, a tablespoon ful of salt and two and a half pounds of brown sugar. When all is well mixed, stir in a quart of sherry and a pint of the best brandy. Mix thoroughly and pack down in a stone crock.

Mince-meat should be prepared several weeks before it is needed, that it may "ripen" and become mellow. Those whose temperance principles forbid the moistening of the mince-meat with brandy or sherry, may use cider in their place. In making mince pies have the best puff-paste. Line pie-plates with this, fill the crust shells with the mince-meat, and lay strips of pastry, lattice-wise, across the tops of the pies. Bake in a good oven, which should be as hot at the bottom as at the top. The pies may be kept for weeks, but must be reheated before serving.

Our New Orleans essayist upon the national pie, is cavalierly disdainful in throwing aside the third variety:

"The barred pie may be dismissed without discussion, being a mere compromise, a pabulum for colorless individuals who are the mugwumps of the dining-room."

In defiance of the slur, I commend my "barred" mince pie, with its latticed cover, as the pearl of the royal race. For a century and a half, the Old Virginia housewives, from whom I proudly claim descent, laid the dainty trellis across the heaving brown breast of the masterpiece, and six generations of epicures have set thereon the seal of their approval.

Pumpkin pie (No. 1)

Belongs to the noble order of the "unkivered" pie.

Add the beaten yolks of four eggs and one cupful of white sugar to two cupfuls of pumpkin that has been stewed and put through a colander. With this mix a quart of milk, one teaspoonful of cinnamon, mace and nutmeg mixed, and the whites of the eggs, beaten stiff. Line a very deep pie-dish with a good paste, cut slashes in it here and there, stir the pumpkin custard well from the bottom and put it into the pastry. Bake in a steady oven.

Pumpkin pie (No. 2)

Into a quart of stewed and strained pumpkin stir a quart of milk, a cup of granulated sugar, cinnamon and nutmeg to taste, and, last of all, five eggs, well beaten. Mix thoroughly, and pour the mixture into a deep pie-plate lined with puff paste. Bake in a good oven until the pumpkin custard is "set." Eat cold. Canned pumpkin is used in the same way and is almost as good as the fresh.

Lemon cream pie (No. 1)

Heat a quart of milk and stir into it one-third of a cupful of prepared flour wet with a little cold milk. Let this get hot, stirring all the while. Beat the yolks of five eggs light with five tablespoonfuls of sugar, and add the milk and flour to this. Let all cook together for one minute after they come to the simmer; take from the fire and add the juice and grated peel of a large lemon. Bake in open shells of puff paste, and, as soon as the custard is set, cover it with a meringue made of the whites of the five eggs beaten stiff with three tablespoonfuls of powdered sugar. Brown lightly and serve cold.

Lemon cream pie (No. 2)

Cream a tablespoonful of butter with a cupful of sugar; dissolve a heaping tablespoonful of corn-starch in a gill of cold water, and stir it into a cupful of boiling water. Stir until smooth; then pour over the sugar and butter. Mix well and when cool stir in the grated rind and the juice of a large lemon, and one beaten egg. Line a pie-plate with puff paste, fill with this mixture and bake. When done, cover with a meringue, and return to the oven just long enough to brown lightly.

Lemon pie with crust

Beat two eggs light and stir into them two cupfuls of sugar; add a pint of water, three tablespoonfuls of cracker-dust, the same quantity of flour rubbed to a paste with a little cold water, the grated rind of one, and the juice of two lemons. Beat hard, add a pinch, each, of cinnamon and nutmeg, and turn the mixture into pie-plates lined with pastry. Cover with an upper crust, cut gashes in this for the escape of the steam, and bake in a steady oven for forty minutes.

Crustless lemon pie

Soak a cupful of crumbs for an hour in a little milk. Cream together a half-cupful of sugar and half as much butter, whip into them the beaten yolks of three eggs and the white of one, reserving the other whites for the meringue. Now add the juice and grated rind of two lemons, then the soaked crumbs. Line a large pie-plate with puff paste, pour in the lemon mixture and bake to a golden brown. Make a meringue of the stiffened whites and two tablespoonfuls of powdered sugar. Draw the pie to the door of the oven, spread with the meringue and return it to the oven just long enough to brown it delicately. Eat cold.

Cocoanut pie

Cream a half-cupful of butter with two scant cupfuls of powdered sugar, and when very light add half a grated cocoanut and a generous tablespoonful of rose-water. Now "fold" in quickly and lightly the stiffened whites of six eggs, turn into a deep pie-dish lined with puff paste and bake in a quick oven. Eat cold with powdered sugar and whipped cream flavored with rose-water. This is delicious.

When it is possible to do so buy the fresh cocoanut and grate it. The prepared or desiccated article put up in boxes may be used as a makeshift. It can never be a worthy substitute for the fresh and juicy nut.

Chocolate pie (No. 1)

Make a custard by pouring two cupfuls of scalding milk gradually upon three eggs that have been beaten well with four tablespoonfuls of sugar. Return to the fire, stir in a half-cupful of grated sweet-chocolate, remove from the fire, add a teaspoonful of vanilla, and pour the mixture into a pie-plate lined with puff paste. Bake until "set."

Chocolate pie (No. 2)

One pint of milk; one cupful of sugar; yolks of two eggs; two tablespoonfuls of grated chocolate. Mix, and bake in an open crust. Make a meringue of the whites of the eggs and a tablespoonful of sugar and spread on the top of the pie to brown.

Orange pie

Rub to a creamy paste a half-cupful of butter and a cupful of granulated sugar. Beat light the yolks of four eggs, whip them into the butter and sugar, add the juice and a quarter of the grated peel of a large orange, a teaspoonful of lemon juice, and the stiffened whites of two eggs. Line a pie-plate with light puff paste and turn the orange mixture into this. Bake until the filling is set and the crust lightly browned. Beat the whites of two eggs light with two tablespoonfuls of powdered sugar. When the pie is done, draw it to the door of the oven, spread it with this meringue, and return to the oven just long enough to color the meringue delicately. Eat cold.

Custard pie

Whip light the yolks of three eggs with four tablespoonfuls of sugar. Pour upon them two cupfuls of boiling milk, stirring this in slowly. Flavor with a teaspoonful of vanilla. Line a pie-plate with paste, brush the inside with the white of an egg, pour in the custard and bake.

Sliced apple pie

Line a deep pie-dish with good puff paste. Put into this peeled and cored and thinly-sliced apples; sprinkle thickly with sugar and squeeze a few drops of lemon juice upon them. Add more sliced apple, more sugar, a little more lemon, and proceed in this way until the dish is full. Cover with a round of puff paste, pinch together the edges of the upper and lower crusts, and cut several slits in the upper to allow the steam to escape. Bake in a steady oven to a golden brown, covering the pie with paper for the first ten minutes.

Creamed sweet apple pie

Pare, core and quarter Campfield pound sweets, or other sweet apples. Put them into a pudding-dish with a few spoonfuls of water to prevent burning, cover closely and cook until tender, but not broken. Add two tablespoonfuls of sugar to each cupful and let them get cold in the syrup. Then cut into thin slices or tiny dice. Roll out some puff paste quite thin; line a pie-plate, sprinkle with flour, lay on another crust and bake until brown. When ready to serve, open the crusts, spread the lower one with the stewed apple, cover with whipped cream, put on the top crust and sprinkle that with powdered sugar.

Creamed apple-sauce pie

Bake your crusts as directed in preceding recipe. When you separate them, spread with well-sweetened apple-sauce beaten light; cover with whipped cream; lay on the upper crust and sprinkle powdered sugar on top.

In both of these recipes you may substitute a meringue of frothed whites, slightly sweetened, for the cream, spreading the same upon the top crust.

Apple meringue pie

Slice and stew ripe, tart apples; run through the colander or vegetable press into a bowl. Sweeten plentifully, and beat in, while hot, a tablespoonful of butter. Have ready buttered pie-plates lined with puff paste; when the sauce is cold fill these shells with it and bake until very lightly browned. Cover with a meringue, slightly sweetened and flavored with vanilla or other essence; set in a hot oven and bake until the meringue begins to color. Sift powdered sugar over all. Eat cold.

Peach meringue pie

Stew and rub peaches through a colander or a vegetable press. Sweeten to taste, and when cold, proceed as directed in last recipe. They are very nice.

Whole peach pie

Line a deep pie-plate with pastry, and lay in it as many whole peeled peaches as it will hold. Strew thickly with sugar; fit on an upper crust and bake to a golden brown. Eat with powdered sugar and cream.

Creamed peach pie (No. 1)

Peel, stone and halve ripe peaches. Line a deep pie-plate with puff paste, and lay the peaches in this. Sprinkle thickly with sugar, and fit on an upper crust. Have ready and cold, a cream sauce. To make this, scald a half-pint of milk and thicken it with a tablespoonful of corn-starch rubbed smooth in a little cold milk. Add two tablespoonfuls of sugar and the frothed white of one egg. Boil together for five minutes and set aside to cool. When the pie is done carefully lift the top crust and fill the pie to overflowing with the cream sauce. Replace the crust and set in a cool place. Sprinkle with powdered sugar and eat very cold.

Creamed peach pie (No. 2)

Bake as above, stoning the peaches and cutting each in half. While hot, insinuate the blade of a knife between upper and lower crust, to loosen them. Let the pie get cold; lift the crust and spread whipped cream upon the peaches. Cover again, strew powdered sugar upon the top crust and eat.

Creamed raspberry pie

Line a pie-dish with good pastry and fill it three-quarters full of red raspberries strewed with granulated sugar. Cover with an upper crust, but rub the edges of this and of the lower crust with butter to prevent their sticking together. Make a cream of a cupful of hot milk thickened with a teaspoonful of corn-starch wet with cold milk. Stir in two tablespoonfuls of sugar, remove from the fire, and when cool whip in the stiffened whites of three eggs. When the pie is done and is cold, lift off the upper crust and cover the raspberries with the "cream." Replace the cover and sift powdered sugar over it.

Cherry pie

Many persons make a cherry pie without stoning the cherries. That stoning them is a trouble is not to be denied, but the result is so satisfactory that it really seems worth while to take the pains to accomplish it. In stoning cherries, use a sharp knife and save all the juice. Grease a deep pie-dish and line it with good puff pastry. Fill the pastry shell with the cherries and the juice that flowed from them in the stoning process. Cover with a thin crust, cut slits in this for the escape of the steam, and bake. Eat cold.

Cranberry pie

Seed a cupful of raisins and chop them into bits. Cut into halves two cupfuls of cranberries and mix them with the minced raisins. Add two even cupfuls of sugar, a cupful of water, two tablespoonfuls of flour and a few drops of lemon juice. Line deep pie-plates with puff paste; fill each with the mixture, put on a thin upper crust and cut slits in this for the escape of the steam. Bake in a good oven to a golden brown. When cold, sprinkle with sugar.

Cranberry and raisin pie

Seed and mince one cupful of raisins; mix with two cupfuls of cranberries halved, a half cupful of water and a cupful of sugar. Stir one teaspoonful of flour with the sugar and mix all well. Fill shells of pastry laid in buttered plates with this mixture, called by some "mock cherry pie," lay strips of crust cut with a jagging-iron over the top and bake.

Strawberry pie

Line a buttered plate with puff paste, wash with white of egg and fill with ripe strawberries capped and washed. Sweeten plentifully, cover with another crust; cut slits in this, and bake.

Currant pie (No. 1)

Mix ripe and stemmed currants with one cupful of sugar to two of currants, and bake between upper and lower crusts. Strew white sugar over the top and eat cold.

Currant pie (No. 2)

Fill a pastry shell with one cupful of ripe currants, cleaned and stemmed. Pour upon them an egg, beaten light with one-half cupful of sugar. Lay another crust over the currants and bake.

New England blueberry pie

Wash and dredge blueberries with flour; then scatter among them half a cupful of sugar for each pint of berries. Fill paste shells with this, dot with butter, cover with another crust and bake.

These are richer than huckleberry or blueberry pies, when made in the usual way, the flour thickening the juice slightly and the butter tempering the acid.

Blackberry pie

Make as directed in foregoing recipe.

Combination berry pie

Line a deep pie-plate with pastry and bake long enough to set the crust on top, but not to brown, or entirely cook it. Have ready a mixture of equal quantities of elderberries and huckleberries with one-fourth as many red currants. Dredge with flour, and sprinkle over all a generous cupful of sugar for a quart of berries; dot the surface with bits of butter,—one tablespoon in all,—cover with a crust which should be well turned under the crust of the lower one, and bake, covered, half an hour, then brown.

Sweet potato pie

Parboil, peel, and when cold, grate enough sweet potatoes to make a pound. Cream a half cupful of butter with three-quarters of a cupful of sugar and the beaten yolks of four eggs, a teaspoonful, each, of powdered cinnamon and nutmeg, the grated potato, the juice and rind of a lemon, a wineglassful of brandy and, last of all, the whites of the eggs. Line a large pie-plate with puff paste, fill with the mixture and bake.

Irish potato pie

Boil and rub through a colander or vegetable press; then proceed as with the sweet potatoes in last recipe, but using a full cupful of sugar.

This pie is even more delicious than the sweet potato compound.

Rhubarb and raisin pie

Peel the rhubarb and cut into inch pieces; pour boiling water over it and let stand for ten minutes. Drain; line the pie-plate with plain paste. Fill the pie with rhubarb, and strew over it one cupful of sugar and one-half cupful of raisins. Add small pieces of butter. Cover with a crust and bake.

Whipped cream pie

(Contributed)

Line a pie-plate with a rich crust and bake in a hot oven. When cool spread over with a layer of jelly or marmalade. Whip one cupful of thick cream, sweetened with powdered sugar, and flavored with vanilla; pour this over the marmalade. Or fill crust with whipped cream to which has been added one teacupful of blanched chopped almonds.

Turnover pies

(Contributed)

Mix a plain puff paste. Roll thin and cut into circular pieces about the size of a saucer. Put fruit over one-half of the piece. Sprinkle with sugar. Wet the edges and turn the paste over. Press the edges together and bake on tins in a quick oven twenty minutes.

Mock mince pie

(Contributed)

Mix well together one cupful of raisins chopped fine, one-half cupful of chopped currants, one-fourth teaspoonful of salt, one tablespoonful of vinegar, two-thirds of a cupful of molasses, one-half cupful of cider, one-half cup of sugar, one-half cupful of cut citron and the juice and rind of two lemons, two Boston crackers rolled and one well-beaten egg. Line a pie-pan with paste and fill with some of the mixture, cover with a puff paste and bake.

Washington pie

(Contributed)

Beat together one tablespoonful of butter, one cupful of sugar and one egg until light. Add one cupful of milk and two cupfuls of flour into which have been sifted one teaspoonful of ginger, one teaspoonful of cinnamon and one-half teaspoonful of baking-powder. Beat thoroughly until smooth. Line the Washington pie-plate with a plain paste, put the mixture into it and bake in a moderate quick oven thirty minutes. When done cover with frosting and set to cool.

Crumb pie

Soak a half cupful of bread-crumbs in enough milk to cover them until they are soft and have absorbed all the milk. Cream a third of a cupful of sugar with two ounces of butter; add two eggs, well beaten, and the juice and grated rind of two small lemons, or one very large one. Now, stir in the soaked crumbs, beat for a minute; turn into a pie-plate lined with puff paste, and bake in a hot oven until brown and very light.

Custard pie

Make a custard by pouring three cupfuls of scalding milk upon four eggs that have been beaten light with four tablespoonfuls of sugar. Flavor with vanilla, and pour into a pie-dish lined with puff paste. Bake until set. Serve cold.

Vinegar pie (No. 1)

One cupful of vinegar; one cupful of water; a tablespoonful of butter; one heaping tablespoonful of flour wet with cold water; two-thirds of a cupful of sugar. Put flour, vinegar, butter and sugar into a saucepan and stir until melted, then add the cold water. Stir until thick. Have pie-tins lined with a rich crust; fill with the mixture and bake for fifteen minutes in a hot oven.

Beat the white of an egg to a stiff meringue, adding two tablespoonfuls of powdered sugar. When the pies are done, draw them to the door of the oven, spread thickly with the meringue, and return to the oven until a very light brown.

Vinegar pie (No. 2)

One egg; one heaping tablespoonful of flour; one teacupful of sugar; one cupful of cold water; one tablespoonful of vinegar; nutmeg to taste. Beat the egg, add the sugar and flour, beating hard; then add the other ingredients, and bake in an open crust.

Currant tarts

Into a quart of sifted flour chop a cupful of firm, cold butter. When the butter is like coarse sand add a cupful of iced water and work into a paste, touching with the hands as little as possi ble. Turn upon a pastry-board and roll out twice; then set on the ice for an hour or two. Line small buttered tart-pans with this paste.

Stem and pick over ripe red currants and wash them. Nearly fill the pastry shells with these and sweeten very generously with granulated sugar. Bake, and, when cold, sprinkle with powdered sugar.

Cranberry tarts

Make a cranberry sauce according to directions already given. Line pâté-pans with puff paste; fill with the cranberry sauce, lay strips of pastry, crosswise, over the tops, and bake in a quick oven. When done, sprinkle with granulated sugar and set away to cool.

Lemon tarts

Cream together a cupful of butter and two cupfuls of sugar, stir in the beaten yolks of six eggs, the grated rind of one, and the juice of two lemons, a dash of nutmeg, a wineglassful of brandy, and the stiffened whites of the eggs. Line pâté-pans with puff paste, and fill with this mixture. Bake in a quick oven and serve cold.

Orange cheese cakes

Peel and seed four large oranges, saving all the juice. Boil half of the peels until tender, and, when cold, beat them to a paste with twice their weight in powdered sugar; add the minced pulp and the juice of the oranges with a tablespoonful of butter; beat all together; line pâté-pans with puff paste, lay in the orange mixture and bake.

There must be no fibrous skin or membrane left in the pulp. To get rid of this rub it through a colander.

Cherry tarts

Wash, stem and stone the cherries. Allow one cupful of sugar to a pint of cherries, if tart fruit be used. Put the sugar and one-half cupful of water on the fire; when boiling add the fruit and cook ten minutes. Stir in one teaspoonful of butter and, if the syrup seem thin, wet one teaspoonful of corn-starch in cold water and stir in to thicken the juice slightly.

Have ready-baked pâtés of pastry; fill with the cherry mixture when the latter is cold, sift sugar over top, and eat.

Fried tartlets

Make a rich puff paste and cut it into pieces six inches square. In the center of each square put a great spoonful of raspberry, strawberry, currant or gooseberry jam. Pinch the four corners of the square together, or fold it in half and pinch the edges tightly together that the fruit may not ooze out. Drop the tarts carefully into a kettle of deep, *boiling* cottolene or other fat, and fry quickly to a delicate brown. Drain in a colander lined with tissue paper.

These are the celebrated "Banbury tarts" of English folk-lore.

HOT PUDDINGS

Boiled puddings

Before attempting a boiled pudding, be sure that you have a good mold with a tightly-fitting cover in which to cook it. You may use such a substitute as a bowl with a floured cloth tied over the top, but this is, at best, a "make-do" which may allow the water to enter and ruin your dough. The best substitute for a mold is a cottolene pail with a top, which may be made more secure by tying it on. Always grease your mold thoroughly,—top, bottom and sides,—and leave room for the swelling of the contents. Three hours will be, as a rule, the longest time required for the boiling of a pudding of ordinary size. All boiled puddings should be served as soon as they are cooked.

Apple pudding (No. 1)

Chop a cupful of suet to a coarse powder and stir it into three cupfuls of flour, twice sifted with a teaspoonful of baking-powder. Add enough milk to make a dough that can be rolled out. Roll into a square sheet. In the center of the sheet lay three cupfuls of peeled and minced apples, strewn with sugar. Bring the four corners of the sheet over the fruit, and pinch the corners together in the middle. Tie up firmly with a piece of broad white tape passed twice around the pudding. Lay in a steamer and cook for two and one-half hours. Remove the tape and serve the pudding with a hard sauce flavored with lemon juice and powdered cinnamon.

Apple pudding (No. 2)

Into two cupfuls of prepared flour chop a tablespoonful of butter, until it is like a coarse yellow powder. Make a batter of this buttered flour, a teacupful of milk and three beaten eggs. Have ready half a dozen peeled and sliced apples, wiped dry, then dredged with flour; stir these into the batter and turn into a greased pudding-mold. Boil for two hours. Eat with a hot lemon sauce.

Cranberry pudding

Sift three cupfuls of flour with a half teaspoonful of salt and stir in a cupful of molasses, a small cupful of sour cream, two beaten eggs and half a teaspoonful of soda dissolved in a little boiling water. Last of all, beat in a cupful and a half of halved cranberries, thoroughly dredged with flour. Turn into a greased mold and steam for at least two hours. Eat with a hard sauce.

Blackberry pudding

Make a batter of a pint of milk, two eggs, and a cupful of flour, sifted with a saltspoonful of salt and a small teaspoonful of baking-powder. Add more flour if the batter is too thin. Beat thoroughly and stir into the batter a pint of blackberries thoroughly dredged with flour. Pour at once into a greased mold and boil for two hours. Serve with a hard sauce.

Plum pudding (No. 1)

Rub together a cupful of granulated sugar and a half cupful of butter. Into this stir a half pound of chopped and powdered suet, then beat in five eggs, a half pint of milk and a teaspoonful of orange juice. Dredge with flour a cupful, each, of seeded raisins and cleaned currants and a half cupful of minced citron. Add this fruit to the batter and stir in a quarter of a teaspoonful, each, of powdered cinnamon, cloves and nutmeg. Last of all, beat in a quart of flour, turn into a large mold and steam for six hours.

Plum pudding (No. 2)

Half a pound, each, of sugar and suet; a quarter of a pound of butter; five cupfuls of flour; one pound, each, of cleaned currants and of raisins; two tablespoonfuls of shredded citron; one cupful of milk; half a teaspoonful, each, of ground mace, cloves and nutmeg; six eggs; half a cupful of brandy.

Rub butter and sugar together and mix with them the milk and the beaten yolks of the eggs. Add the flour and the whipped whites; dredge the raisins (which should have been seeded and chopped), the currants and citron with flour, and put these in with the spices and the brandy. Mix well, pack into a greased mold, plunge at once into a pot of boiling water and boil five hours. Be careful that the water does not boil over the top of the mold and get into the pudding.

Fig pudding (No. 1)

Soak a cupful of bread-crumbs in a cupful of milk for half an hour. Chop enough suet to make a quarter of a cupful; beat three eggs light; cut into tiny bits a sufficient number of soaked figs to make a cupful of the minced fruit.

Turn the soaked crumbs into a bowl, and stir into them a half cupful of granulated sugar, the whipped eggs, the powdered suet, a pinch of salt and a dash, each, of cinnamon and nutmeg. Last of all, stir in the minced figs thickly dredged with flour, beat well and turn into a greased pudding mold with a closely-fitting top. Boil for about three hours. Turn out and eat with a hard sauce.

www.ingramcontent.com/pod-product-compliance
Lightning Source LLC
Chambersburg PA
CBHW081722100526
44591CB00016B/2471